Jessica Elliott Dennison

simple,
delicious
recipes
using
pantry
staples

TIN CAN
MAGIC

Hardie Grant
B O O K S

Photography by Matt Russell

CONTENTS

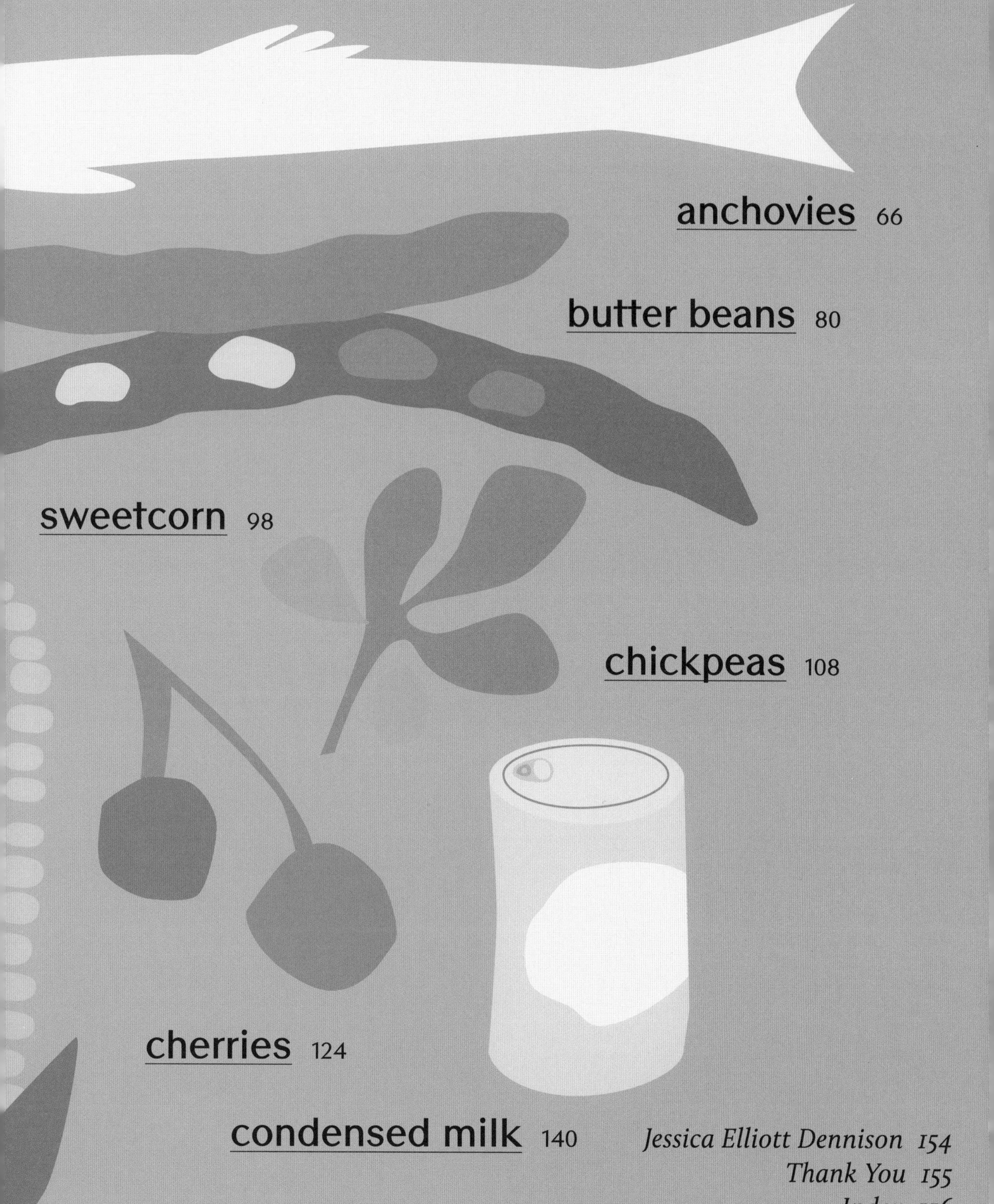

THE MAGIC OF TINS

The idea for this book is pretty simple; it's an everyday guide for transforming those trusty tin cans from the back of your cupboard into something special. I've developed a relaxed approach to cooking and socialising over food, and these recipes offer realistic guidance on how you can pull together straightforward yet interesting meals using easy-to-find ingredients, many of which are likely to already be in your cupboard.

I don't consider myself a chef. I am a cook. These days, most of my hours are spent cooking in the kitchen of 27 Elliott's: my neighbourhood cafe, supperclub and workshop space in Edinburgh. There, led by the season's produce and my local suppliers, I chalk up a weekly menu on the blackboard. In dark January, it's forced rhubarb that features heavily, sometimes poached in blood orange until releasing bright pink juices, then spooned over strained yoghurt and roasted hazelnuts (filberts) for breakfast, or with brown sugar meringues in the afternoon. As we enter spring, purple-sprouting broccoli and wild garlic take centre stage, topping warm plates of sausage braised chickpeas (garbanzos) and fried eggs on toast for the weekend brunch crowd. As the colder months creep back in, it's the variety of pumpkins that are championed — lazily roasted with lemon and garlic until caramelised then thrown over green lentils and some roughly torn herbs in time for the lunch rush.

But despite getting overly excited about each season's produce, it's the trusty storecupboard tins and cans that form the backbone of my everyday cooking: both in the cafe and when cooking at home with friends and my husband, Philip. It's the tin of coconut milk I reach for to make a dahl or quick curry mid-week (pages 18 and 54), the tin of chopped tomatoes that comes together perfectly with butter and some comforting fettuccine (page 41) and the cherries sitting in their tin juices, ready to be thrown over a rustic frangipane galette (page 134) that are the true heroes of my kitchen.

The recipe I'm asked for most at 27 Elliott's is 'the beans' (page 91). The dish simply begins by frying onions, garlic and sage. Then as you pour in white wine and tinned butter (lima) beans – tin juice and all – something pretty magical happens. The whole lot reduces down together, transforming into an indulgent yet humble plate of food, one which my regulars love to mop up with toasted sourdough. At times when you've got loads of fresh herbs to hand, you can quickly stir them into a vinegary salsa verde then spoon over the beans too, taking the whole thing in a punchier direction (page 93). On chillier days, if you switch the sage for fennel, and the white wine for red, you end up with an even heartier, more comforting meal than the original white version (page 92). Throughout *Tin Can Magic* I've offered some of the recipes, such as the braised butter beans (page 89) in this manner – three different ways. This is to illustrate just how versatile and interesting storecupboard staples such as beans, lentils and chickpeas can really be by slightly tweaking and riffing on a recipe, using the herbs and spices you already have to hand.

In keeping with my first book, *Salad Feasts*, I've included a list of substitutes with each of the recipes, hopefully making them more flexible and hard-working for you. I've also marked estimate cooking times, giving you an idea of how long each will realistically take to prepare. Most of them you'll easily have on the table in under 25 minutes, such as the Chilled Chilli Tomato Noodles (page 49) and the Garlic Mushroom Lentils (page 13). Some, such as the Cauliflower, Sweet Potato and Chickpea Traybake (page 122) need slightly longer, as their flavours develop by simmering on the stove or roasting in a hot oven. However, I promise there's minimal hands-on faff or complicated

techniques involved. With many of the recipes I've included feast ideas; these are simple suggestions for complementary sides, small plates and drinks, for times when you want to pull together an even larger feast. There are also plenty of cook's tips dotted throughout; these offer guidance for fixing something when it goes slightly wrong, what to do on occasions when you're missing a key ingredient, or ideas on what to make with any leftovers the next day. The recipes have all kindly been tested by friends living in different countries to me, where the availability of ingredients differs, along with their individual cooking abilities. So hopefully they inspire your day-to-day cooking while feeling very much do-able.

While I, of course, dream of one day owning a walk-in pantry filled with every exotic storecupboard ingredient imaginable, I realise that's not how most of us actually live. Instead, my hope is that *Tin Can Magic* stays out on your kitchen worktop, serving as a relaxed everyday resource for utilising those basic staples in your storecupboard. Getting the ones you love round the table for a simple meal and glass of wine, while making the most of what's already to hand, is really satisfying. So dust off those tins and happy cooking!

JESS

@FOODJESS

HOW TO
TRANSFORM
A TIN

The brilliant thing about having a few staple tins in your cupboard is that you're never far away from rustling up a quick, simple meal.

In developing these recipes, I've tried to consider how you can easily add contrasting textures, colours and flavours to make your own everyday cooking more interesting. These are some things to in keep in mind:

1) PICK YOUR HERO TIN

Which tin has been sitting in the back of your cupboard for a while that needs using up? How can you cook it to make it the centrepiece of a simple feast? Perhaps it's a pulse that can be rinsed in fresh water to become the basis of a salad? Or could it be charred in a hot pan to become a smoky taco filling? Perhaps it suits being slowly braised with lots of woody herbs and wine to become a warm, comforting supper? Have a think about which direction you'd like the meal to go in.

2) ADD 2-3 FRESH INGREDIENTS

Consider how a few fresh ingredients could enhance and contrast with your chosen tin. If you're working with corn that's naturally sweet for example, think about teaming it with fragrant herbs or something more zingy and punchy like lemon rather than another sweet ingredient.

3) SOME INTERESTING CONTRAST

This is where everyday salted cheeses like feta and halloumi come in, or even just a cooling spoonful of strained yoghurt if it's a spicy curry or dahl you're making. Try to think how you can balance your hero tin; earthy beetroots contrast nicely with sweet tinned cherries in a salad, for example.

4) CRUNCH AND ADDED TEXTURE

A handful of toasted nuts, seeds or whole spice can really help lift softer tinned ingredients such as lentils, chickpeas and beans. Have a look round your cupboard and see what you can use up to give your meals another layer of texture.

A FEW NOTES ON THE RECIPES

Each of the recipes have been designed with relaxed, everyday cooking in mind. You'll notice they all include substitute ingredients and estimate prep times along with ideas for transforming individual dishes into an even larger feast.

With many of the recipes you'll find my commentary on when to buy ingredients at their best and most affordable, what to do with any leftovers (the ragù on page 25, for example, is fantastic when turned into a soup for lunch the next day) and how to fix any cooking steps that go slightly wrong – rescuing a split aioli you've made to go with the Sausage and Spinach Braised Lentils on page 30, for example.

INGREDIENT SUBSTITUTES

You'll spot a list of alternative ingredient ideas with the majority of the recipes – these are designed to make your everyday cooking really flexible and easy, no matter the season or availability of shops near you. Perhaps I've fried off an interesting variety of wild mushroom, but you can't get your hands on the same ones in your local express store; just use regular white button mushrooms with the suggested splash of soy sauce to get a similar deep, earthy flavour instead. Or perhaps I've roasted cauliflower to top a dahl, but cauliflowers are just not your thing. Chop a broccoli, some Brussels sprouts or even a cabbage instead. Use the recipe as a loose guide, get a feel for the method, standout textures and flavours, then make it your own. Follow your instincts and you'll be onto something delicious.

FEAST IDEAS

I've written the recipes in their simplest form, with time-short, tired mid-week cooking in mind. However, many of the dishes lend themselves to being part of an even larger weekend feast; perhaps when there are more people around to feed or when you've got a bit more time to potter in the kitchen and reach for a few more ingredients. The Whipped Butter Bean Dip (page 83), for example, can be whipped up in minutes and spread over toast or with some oven-roasted veggies mid-week, but serve it with the Za'atar Roasted Chicken (page 86), some charred little gem lettuce (bibb lettuce), a few flatbreads and quick pickles alongside some good wine on the weekend, and you're onto an absolute crowd-pleasing feast.

KIT FOR SIMPLE COOKING

As space is pretty tight in both my home and cafe kitchens, I like to keep equipment minimal yet hard-working. Investing in the tools you reach for on a daily basis can make cooking far more enjoyable. A good knife and sharpener are game-changing for safe, confident chopping; my favourite is an all-rounder one by Japanese brand Tadafusa. A quality speed peeler, grater, Microplane fine zester, food processor and frying or griddle pan (skillet) are also really helpful. A mandolin isn't an absolute must, but is great for finely shaving vegetables, especially ones that can be turned into a quick pickle.

GREEN

ENTILS

GARLIC MUSHROOM LENTILS AND FRIED EGGS

with Parmesan and Rosemary

20 minutes

4 tablespoons rapeseed (canola),
    vegetable or light olive oil
3 garlic cloves, peeled and finely sliced
200 g (7 oz) mushrooms, dirt brushed
    off, roughly torn (ideally a mix of
    wild, chestnut and button)
2 sprigs of rosemary, leaves only,
    roughly chopped
1 x 390 g (13¾ oz) tin of green lentils
    in water, drained and rinsed
½ lemon, zest and juice
1 teaspoon salt
100 g (3½ oz) spinach, washed
    and drained
2 eggs
4 tablespoons finely grated Parmesan

SUBSTITUTES

Rosemary
sage, tarragon, thyme

Green lentils
cooked puy lentils, cooked pearl
barley, cooked spelt, cooked
brown rice

Parmesan
pecorino, feta, goat's cheese, mature
Cheddar, halloumi

Walnuts
almonds, hazelnuts, pecans

The key to frying mushrooms is allowing your pan to get smoking hot so that they catch at the edges and take on an almost meaty, charred flavour. Keep an eye out for more unusual wild varieties to mix in with more common button and chestnut mushrooms – they're increasingly available and offer a deeper flavour and more interesting textures.

∗ First, heat 2 tablespoons of oil in a large non-stick frying pan (skillet) over a medium heat. Add the garlic and, stirring regularly, fry for 1–2 minutes until golden and fragrant. Take care not to burn the garlic or it will become overly bitter. Transfer the garlic to a small bowl and set aside.

∗ Next, increase the heat to high and add 1 tablespoon more oil. Add the mushrooms and cook for 4 minutes, or until browning and catching at the edges. Stir in the rosemary, fry for 1–2 minutes until crisp and fragrant. Stir in the lentils, lemon juice, salt and spinach until wilted. Add a few splashes of water if the pan contents look a bit dry.

∗ Heat 1 tablespoon of oil in another non-stick frying pan over a high heat. Crack in the eggs and fry for 1–2 minutes until crisp on the base but still with a runny yolk, or to your liking.

———— To assemble

Divide the mushroomy-lentils between two plates. Top with a fried egg and the reserved crispy garlic. Sprinkle over the Parmesan and the zest of the remaining lemon half.

COOK'S TIP

If you can't find more interesting varieties of mushrooms, add a splash of soy sauce when you stir in the spinach, as this will give them a deeper, earthier flavour.

GREEN LENTILS

SPINACH, DILL AND GOAT'S CHEESE LENTIL FRITTERS

SERVES 4
(MAKES 12 FRITTERS)

30 minutes

100 g (3½ oz) spinach
large bunch of dill fronds
1 x 390 g (13¾ oz) tin of green lentils
    in water, drained and rinsed
85 g (3 oz) sourdough, blitzed
    into breadcrumbs
2 eggs
75 g (2½ oz) goat's cheese, grated
    (shredded)
grated zest of 1 lemon, the fruit then
    cut into wedges
150 ml (5 fl oz/scant ⅔ cup) rapeseed
    (canola), vegetable or light olive oil,
    plus extra if needed
sea salt flakes

SUBSTITUTES

Spinach
chard, spring greens, kale

Dill
flat-leaf parsley, basil

Lentils
chickpeas (garbanzos), butter (lima)
beans, kidney beans

Goat's cheese
feta, halloumi, Cheddar, salted ricotta

Once you get the hang of making fritters, they can become such a good staple to rustle up from just a handful of ingredients. It's incredible how these ones stretch a regular tin of lentils into a crowd-pleasing meal. I've used goat's cheese for a slight tang, but you could easily use feta, halloumi or some Cheddar if that's what you've got in the refrigerator. Likewise, play about with the herbs and greens to suit.

The key to a crispy-edged fritter that doesn't fall apart is a touch of bravery. Test your oil is hot and bubbling with a pinch of the mixture before frying the whole batch, and refrain from moving them about too much as this allows them to develop a dark, crisp exterior.

* First, pour 400 ml (13 fl oz/generous 1½ cups) water into a large, deep frying pan (skillet), bring to the boil over a high heat, then throw in the spinach and dill and simmer for 2–3 minutes, or until the greens have wilted. Drain, rinse under plenty of cold water, then roughly chop.

* Next, transfer the chopped dill and spinach to a food processor. Add the lentils, breadcrumbs, eggs, goat's cheese and lemon zest, then gently pulse until combined. Try not to over-blend as you want to keep some nice texture for the fritters, not end up with a lentil smoothie. Shape the mixture into 12 patties (roughly a large heaped tablespoon each) then set aside on a plate.

* Rinse out and dry the frying pan, then add the oil and heat over a medium-high heat. Line a few plates with kitchen paper. Test the oil is hot enough by adding a small pinch of the fritter mixture to the pan. If it sizzles and bubbles, you're ready for frying. Gently add the fritters to fit the pan (lay them away from you) and cook for 3–4 minutes each side, or until crisp on the edges. Using a slotted spoon or fish slice, transfer the fritters to the lined plates to soak up any excess oil, then sprinkle the salt over the top. Repeat until the mixture is all cooked, adding more fresh oil to the pan if necessary.

———— To assemble

Pile up three fritters on each plate, sprinkle over a pinch more salt, then serve with a lemon wedge for squeezing over.

THREE WAYS

LENTIL DAHL

A quick dahl is probably the thing Philip and I cook more than anything on busy weeknights, so here I'm showing you how to take it in a few different flavour directions by using different spices from the back of your storecupboard, along with whichever vegetables you have to hand. The carrot one offers a nice ginger and cumin hit; the tomato one is sourer and fresher; and the cauliflower and coconut one is the most creamy and comforting.

Each serve two very generously when eaten on its own from a big bowl, or four people when eaten with bread or rice. You'll notice I ask you to toast your whole dried spices for a minute or two before stirring into the onion base; you'll get way more intensity that way.

While the dahl is simmering, you can make the Garlic Salted Yoghurt and/or the Frying Pan Flatbreads (page 18). If the breads feel like a step too far, try charring some slices of sourdough over an open flame for a lovely wood-oven flavour.

If I'm making this dahl feast for friends coming round, I'll often make the lentils the day before then just reheat with a few splashes of water while the flatbreads are cooking. The yoghurt is an easy one to delegate too!

1 CARROT AND TOASTED
CUMIN LENTIL DAHL

2 ROASTED CAULIFLOWER
AND COCONUT LENTIL DAHL

3 TOMATO AND CHILLI
LENTIL DAHL

Optional Sides

GARLIC SALTED YOGHURT
FRYING PAN FLATBREAD
(BOTH ON PAGE 18)

1 CARROT AND TOASTED CUMIN LENTIL DAHL

SERVES 2 VERY GENEROUSLY
(OR 4 WITH FLATBREAD)

45 minutes

2 teaspoons cumin seeds
5 tablespoons rapeseed (canola),
    vegetable or light olive oil
3 onions, peeled and finely sliced
4 garlic cloves, peeled and finely sliced
2 teaspoons ground cumin
¼ teaspoon chilli (hot pepper) flakes
½ teaspoon ground turmeric
1 teaspoon ground coriander
1 x 390 g (13¾ oz) tin of green lentils
    in water
1 x 400 ml (14 fl oz) tin of coconut milk
2 teaspoons salt, plus extra to taste
thumb-sized piece of fresh ginger
    root, peeled
3 carrots, peeled
grated zest of ½ lemon
small bunch of coriander (cilantro),
    dill or mint (optional)

Frying Pan Flatbreads

250 g (9 oz/2 cups) plain
    (all-purpose) flour,
    plus extra for rolling out
1 teaspoon baking powder
1 teaspoon sea salt flakes
250 g (9 oz/1 cup) strained yoghurt
    (ideally full-fat)
rapeseed (canola), light olive or
    vegetable oil for frying

Garlic Salted Yoghurt

½ garlic clove, peeled and minced
5 tablespoons strained yoghurt,
    ideally full fat
½ teaspoon sea salt flakes
grated zest of ½ lemon
1 tablespoon rapeseed (canola) oil

* First, heat a wide non-stick pan on high. Add the cumin seeds then dry-fry for 1–2 minutes until fragrant. Transfer to a pestle and mortar or cutting board, then roughly crush.

* Next, add the oil to the pan along with the onion and garlic. Reduce the heat to low, then fry for 16–18 minutes until soft. Add the crushed cumin seeds, ground cumin, chilli flakes, turmeric and coriander, then stir for 2–3 minutes until fragrant. Pour in the lentils, including the tin water, coconut milk and salt.

* Using a Microplane zester or fine side of a box grater, grate in the ginger; discard the tough root. Coarsely grate the carrots, then add to the lentils along with the lemon zest. Simmer for 10 minutes, stirring regularly, then taste for seasoning; you may want to add more salt.

* While the dahl is cooking, make the flatbreads. First, stir the flour, baking powder, salt and yoghurt together in a large mixing bowl until combined. Dust a few handfuls of flour onto your worktop, then knead the dough for 1–2 minutes until smooth.

* Preheat a wide frying pan (skillet) over a high heat until smoking then, using a rolling pin or rounded bottle, roll the dough into four rough flatbreads, around 18 cm (7 in) in diameter. Drizzle a few tablespoons of oil into the hot pan (take care as it will be incredibly hot), then lay a flatbread in the pan and cook for 2 minutes without interfering. Carefully using tongs, flip the flatbreads and fry for a further 2 minutes, or until charred at the edges and puffing up in the middle. Repeat until all the dough is cooked. You may need to reduce the heat to medium once you've done a flatbread or two.

* To make the garlic salted yoghurt, stir together all the ingredients until smooth.

——— To assemble

Spoon the lentils onto two plates. Pick over the fresh herbs, then cut the zested lemon into two and place a wedge on each plate. Serve with the flatbreads and a spoon of Garlic Salted Yoghurt, if you like.

SUBSTITUTES

Onions
spring onions (scallions), leeks,
red onions

Carrots
pumpkin, squash, swede, parsnips

Cumin seeds
mustard seeds, curry leaf, fennel seeds

COOK'S TIP

If you've got extra carrots to use up, roast them whole
with a splash of oil in a very hot oven while the dahl is
simmering, then serve alongside for additional texture
(as photographed).

ROASTED CAULIFLOWER AND COCONUT LENTIL DAHL

SERVES 2 VERY GENEROUSLY
(OR 4 WITH FLATBREAD)

45 minutes

1 cauliflower, outer stems removed,
    cut into small wedges through
    the core
5 tablespoons rapeseed (canola),
    vegetable or light olive oil
3 teaspoons sea salt flakes
2 teaspoons ground turmeric
2 teaspoons cumin seeds
1½ teaspoons fenugreek seeds
3 onions, peeled and finely sliced
4 garlic cloves, peeled and
    finely sliced
2 teaspoons garam masala
1 teaspoon chilli (hot pepper) flakes
1 teaspoon ground cumin
1 x 390 g (13¾ oz) tin of green lentils
    in water
1 x 400 ml (14 fl oz) tin of
    coconut milk (ideally full-fat)
grated zest of 1 lemon

OPTIONAL SIDES

Frying Pan Flatbreads (page 18)
Garlic Salted Yoghurt (page 18)

SUBSTITUTES

Cauliflower
broccoli, Brussels sprouts,
sweetheart cabbage

Onions
spring onions (scallions), leeks,
red onions

Coconut milk
coconut cream, pinch of brown sugar

Fenugreek seeds
mustard seeds, curry leaf,
fennel seeds

* First, preheat the oven to 190°C (375°F/Gas 5), then toss the cauliflower, 2 tablespoons of rapeseed oil, 1 teaspoon each of salt and turmeric together in a tray. Roast for 25–30 minutes until catching at the edges, shaking the tray halfway through.

* Meanwhile, heat a wide non-stick pan over a high heat. Add the cumin and fenugreek seeds, then dry-fry for 1–2 minutes until fragrant. Set aside.

* Next, add 3 tablespoons of oil to the pan along with the onion and garlic. Reduce the heat to low, then fry for 16–18 minutes until soft. Add the toasted cumin and fenugreek seeds, garam masala, chilli flakes and ground cumin, then stir for 2–3 minutes until fragrant. Pour in the lentils, including the tin water, coconut milk, lemon zest and 2 teaspoons salt and remaning turmeric. Increase the heat and allow to simmer, stirring regularly for 10 minutes then taste for seasoning; you may want to add more salt.

——— To assemble

Spoon the lentils onto two plates. Pile over the roasted cauliflower, then cut the zested lemon into wedges for squeezing over. Serve with the flatbreads and a spoon of Garlic Salted Yoghurt, if you fancy.

COOK'S TIP

If you've got a red onion or some radishes to hand, finely slice, then quickly pickle them in a few splashes of vinegar, a pinch of sugar and salt while the lentils are simmering. You could also throw in a few handfuls of spinach just before serving for extra greenery.

3 TOMATO AND CHILLI LENTIL DAHL

with Quick Tomato and Lime Pickle

SERVES 2 VERY GENEROUSLY
(OR 4 WITH FLATBREAD)

45 minutes

5 tablespoons rapeseed (canola),
   vegetable or light olive oil
2 teaspoons mustard seeds
3 onions, peeled and finely sliced
4 garlic cloves, peeled and
   finely sliced
3 teaspoons ground cumin
2 teaspoons chilli (hot pepper) flakes
2 teaspoons garam masala
1 x 390 g (13¾ oz) tin of green lentils
   in water
1 x 400 ml (14 fl oz) tin of coconut
   milk (ideally full-fat)
1 x 400 g (14 oz) tin of chopped
   tomatoes
2 teaspoons salt, plus extra to taste

Quick Tomato and Lime Pickle
100 g (3½ oz) ripe tomatoes, at room
   temp, roughly sliced (aim for
   random shapes, not perfect cubes)
1 spring onion (scallion), finely sliced
   (optional)
juice of ½ lime
½ teaspoon sugar
⅛ teaspoon sea salt flakes

OPTIONAL SIDES

Frying Pan Flatbreads (page 18)
Garlic Salted Yoghurt (page 18)

SUBSTITUTES

Fresh tomatoes
radishes, cucumber

Onions
spring onions (scallions), leeks,
red onions

Coconut milk
coconut cream, pinch of brown sugar

* To make the Quick Tomato and Lime Pickle, stir the ingredients together in a small bowl. Set aside to lightly pickle.

* Next, to make the dahl, heat the oil in a wide saucepan over high heat, add the mustard seeds, onion and garlic. Take care as the mustard seeds will pop and dance around the pan a bit. Reduce the heat to low then fry for 16–18 minutes until soft. Add the ground cumin, chilli flakes and garam masala then stir for 2–3 minutes until fragrant.

* Pour in the lentils, including the tin water, coconut milk, tinned tomatoes and salt. Increase the heat and allow to simmer, stirring regularly for 15 minutes. Using a potato masher or fish slice, pulp the tomatoes to remove any big chunks, then taste for seasoning; you may want to add more salt.

——— To assemble

Spoon the lentils between two plates. Spoon over the fresh Quick Tomato and Lime Pickle, along with a few splashes of the pickling juices. Serve with the flatbreads and a spoon of Garlic Salted Yoghurt, if you fancy.

COOK'S TIP

When they're in-season and in abundance, try swapping the tinned tomatoes for fresh ones in the dahl as well as the pickle.

YOGHURT, LENTIL AND DILL SOUP

SERVES 2

20 minutes

2 tablespoons butter (salted
   or unsalted)
1 tablespoon rapeseed (canola),
   vegetable or light olive oil
1 onion, peeled and finely sliced
1 teaspoon dried mint leaves
1 egg
150 g (5 oz/⅔ cup) strained yoghurt
   (ideally full-fat)
1 teaspoon sea salt flakes,
   plus extra to taste
1 x 390 g (13¾ oz) tin of green lentils
   in water, rinsed and drained
handful of dill fronds
handful of mint leaves
grated zest of ½–1 lemon

SUBSTITUTES

Onion
spring onions (scallions),
leek, fennel, shallot

Dill/mint
flat-leaf parsley, tarragon

It might sound slightly odd having warm yoghurt in a soup, but I promise it's delicious and ideal on those turn-of-the-summer days when you still want something bright, fresh and herby but also slightly warming and comforting.

* First, melt the butter and oil in a medium frying pan (skillet), add the onion and dried mint, then fry on low for 8–10 minutes until soft; take care not to burn the onions.

* Meanwhile, using a fork, whisk the egg, yoghurt and salt in a small bowl.

* Once the onions is soft, remove from the heat and allow to cool for a minute or so. Stir in 4 tablespoons of the yoghurt mixture, 1 spoonful at a time, until warm and incorporated. Don't be tempted to skip this step or the yoghurt will split if you pour it all in at once. Stir in the remaining yoghurt mixture, along with 100 ml (3½ fl oz/scant ½ cup) of water and the lentils, then gently heat on the lowest heat. Tear in most of the herbs, zest of half the lemon then taste for salt; you may want to add more salt and/or lemon zest.

———— To assemble

Divide into two bowls, then scatter the reserved herbs over the top and eat immediately while still warm.

FEAST TIP

If you wanted to turn the soup into a larger dinner, serve with the Frying Pan Flatbreads (see page 18), topped with slices of in-season, ripe tomatoes, some finely chopped flat-leaf parsley, a zesting of lemon and a splash of your favourite oil.

GREEN LENTILS

LENTIL RAGÙ AND RICOTTA ORECCHIETTE

SERVES 6
(IDEAL FOR BATCH COOKING)

1 hour

250 g (9 oz) tub ricotta (ideally full-fat)
5 tablespoons rapeseed (canola),
    vegetable or light olive oil
2 carrots, peeled and finely diced
1 onion, peeled and finely diced
1 celery stalk, peeled and finely diced
2 bay leaves (optional)
3 teaspoons sea salt flakes
2 garlic cloves, peeled and minced
½ teaspoon chilli (hot pepper) flakes
300 ml (10 fl oz/1¼ cups) red wine
2 x 390 g (14 oz) tins of green lentils
    in water
1 x 400 g (14 oz) tin of chopped
    tomatoes
450 g (1 lb) orecchiette
100 g (3½ oz) Parmesan (optional)
freshly ground black pepper

SUBSTITUTES

Ricotta
burrata, buffalo mozzarella,
goat's curd

Celery stalk/onion/carrot
fennel, leek, spring onions (scallions)

Orecchiette
any other pasta shape

Red wine
white wine, stock or water with
a splash of vinegar

This is hearty comfort food, straight from the back of your cupboard, inspired by an Italian-style ragù. Orecchiette is my go-to pasta shape of choice for this, as I love how the lentil sauce sits so nicely in the little al dente 'ears', but of course just use whichever pasta you've got to hand. You'll notice this feeds up to six people; the idea is you throw together a big pot of this, either to feed a large crowd with a bottle of red wine and minimal stress, or to keep in the refrigerator for a few days where the flavours will continue to intensify.

* First, drain the ricotta in a sieve (fine mesh strainer) over a bowl or sink. Next, heat the oil in a large, wide pan over a medium heat. Add the carrots, onion, celery stalk, bay leaves and salt, then fry for 10 minutes until beginning to pick up colour and soften. Stir in the garlic and chilli flakes, fry for 2 minutes until fragrant then pour in the wine. Increase the heat to high to allow some of the alcohol to burn off, then using a spoon or spatula, scrape up any sticky bits from the bottom of the pan. Pour in the lentils, including the tin juice, the tomatoes and one and a half tins' worth of fresh water, then simmer the mixture over a high heat for half an hour until thickened and reduced. Using a fish slicer or potato masher, crush down a quarter of the sauce (this will help thicken it further) then taste for seasoning.

* After 20 minutes of the sauce simmering, bring a large saucepan of water to the boil, then throw in the pasta and simmer on a rolling boil until al dente – check the packet for exact cooking times. Reserve a mugful of starchy cooking water, then drain. Stir the cooked pasta through the sauce, adding in splashes of cooking water if needed to ensure all the pasta is nicely coated.

——— To assemble

Divide the pasta among the plates, gently break over nuggets of ricotta, then finely grate the Parmesan over the top, plus plenty of freshly ground black pepper.

FEAST TIP

This pasta lends itself to a big social dinner with some nice red wine. Braised greens with chopped anchovy and lemon make a beautiful side dish, or you could char some little gem lettuce (bibb lettuce) as per page 101 topped with finely grated (shredded) Parmesan.

COOK'S TIP

You could transform this ragù into a hearty soup the next day by topping up with water or stock and a handful of greens, such as spinach, kale or chard.

ROASTED PUMPKIN LENTILS

with Burnt Garlic Yoghurt and Lemon

45 minutes

1 small pumpkin or squash (sweet
    varieties like coquina, butternut,
    onion, kabocha and acorn squash
    all work well)
3 tablespoons rapeseed (canola),
    vegetable or olive oil
1 teaspoon sea salt flakes
1 lemon, cut into 4 rough wedges
1 garlic bulb, sliced through the
    middle equator
handful of dill fronds
handful of flat-leaf parsley leaves
handful of mint leaves
1 x 390 g (13¾ oz) tin of green lentils
    in water
5 tablespoons strained yoghurt
    (ideally full-fat)

SUBSTITUTES

Tinned lentils
tinned chickpeas (garbanzos), ready-
cooked lentil sachet

Pumpkin
carrots, cauliflower, beetroot (beet)

Dill/flat-leaf parsley/mint
basil, shredded spring onion (scallion)

One of my favourite times to cook is early autumn, when the variety of weird and wonderful-looking pumpkins become a constant of my kitchen. Here I roast the pumpkin in its skin, partly because it's delicious when slightly catching from the heat of the oven, but mostly because peeling it involves far too much faff!

If you're looking for lunchbox ideas, this is a great one for making extra for dinner then packing up for lunch the next day. Just make sure you allow it to return to room temperature before tucking in.

* First, heat the oven to 200°C (400°F/Gas 7). Halve the pumpkin, scoop out and discard the seeds then cut into chunky wedges (don't bother peeling it). Put the pumpkin in a large roasting tin, then toss with 2 tablespoons of oil, salt, lemon wedges and garlic (ensuring the exposed garlic is lightly oiled). Roast for 25 minutes, remove the garlic, then roast for a further 10 minutes, or until the pumpkin is completely soft and beginning to catch at the edges.

* Meanwhile, finely chop the herbs, then stir through the drained lentils in a large bowl along with 1 tablespoon of oil.

* Carefully using a fork, or once cool enough to handle with fingers, crush three of the caramelised garlic cloves into a pulp. Stir together with the yoghurt in a small bowl.

——— To assemble

Divide the herby lentils onto two plates. Pile up with the roasted pumpkin, squeeze over the caramelised lemon, then dollop over the roasted garlic yoghurt to finish.

GREEN LENTILS

COOK'S TIP

For added crunch, toast then crush a handful of hazelnuts, walnuts or almonds and sprinkle over before serving.

1 SAUSAGE AND SPINACH
BRAISED LENTILS

2 CARROT AND THYME
SAUSAGE BRAISED
LENTILS

3 FENNEL AND RED WINE
SAUSAGE BRAISED
LENTILS

THREE WAYS

SAUSAGE BRAISED LENTILS

A take on these Sausage Braised Lentils is a go-to lunch dish at 27 Elliott's, providing much-needed comfort throughout Edinburgh's chillier months. I play about with the base herbs, wine and type of aioli to suit what our local suppliers have delivered that week. It's a good recipe to have up your sleeve at home, too, as it's so easily adaptable to work with what's already in the fridge.

The wild garlic and spinach feel very much springtime-British; the carrot, thyme and white wine lentils are definitely French-inspired; while the fennel and red wine version feel more rustic Italian nonna-style.

Please don't feel intimated by the thought of making your own aioli – you can easily whisk it up in minutes, and once you've got the hang of it, you can thrown in extra herbs to really make it your own to serve with other simple dishes, including roasted chicken, grilled (broiled) fish and charred vegetables. I like using rapeseed (canola) oil to make our aioli as it gives a vibrant yellow colour and is grown and pressed locally to us, but of course, use a light olive oil if that's what you've got to hand. And if I still haven't convinced you to make your own aioli, the Sausage Braised Lentils are meal-worthy just as they are!

SAUSAGE AND SPINACH BRAISED LENTILS

with Wild Garlic Aioli

SERVES 2 GENEROUSLY (OR 4 WHEN
EATEN WITH BREAD AND/OR SALAD)

1 hour, 15 minutes

4 tablespoons rapeseed (canola),
    vegetable or light olive oil
1 fennel, finely sliced, fronds reserved
1 onion, peeled and finely sliced
1 large carrot, peeled and finely sliced
    on an angle
a few sprigs of rosemary, leaves only
1 teaspoon sea salt flakes, plus extra
    to taste
3 garlic cloves, peeled and
    finely sliced
4 good-quality pork sausages
200 ml (7 fl oz/scant 1 cup) white wine
1 x 390 g (13¾ oz) tin of green lentils
    in water
100 g (3½ oz) spinach, washed
    and drained

Wild Garlic Aioli

1 egg yolk
1½ teaspoons Dijon mustard
½ garlic clove, peeled and minced
1 teaspoon sea salt flakes
juice and grated zest of ½ lemon
300 ml (10 fl oz/1¼ cups) rapeseed
    (canola) oil, in a jug for easy pouring
handful of wild garlic, washed and
    rinsed, finely chopped, flowers
    reserved (optional)

SUBSTITUTES

Fennel
leek, celery stalks

Rosemary
thyme, sage

Sausages
minced (ground) pork or chicken

Wild garlic
basil, tarragon

When wild garlic is in-season, their leaves are lovely blended into an aioli to top these braised lentils. If you can't get hold of any, just follow the recipe as is and you'll still have a bright, garlicky version.

* First, heat 3 tablespoons of oil in a large, wide non-stick frying pan (skillet). Add the fennel, onion, carrot, rosemary, salt and garlic then fry over a medium heat for 10–15 minutes until soft and beginning to turn golden brown.

* Once they're golden and soft, transfer the vegetables to a plate, then increase the heat to high. Next, score each sausage down the middle of its skin and squeeze out the meat into the hot frying pan (discard the skins). Add in 1 tablespoon more oil then fry for 6–8 minutes, using a wooden spoon to crush the meat into rough, large mince. Don't worry about any bits that are catching or burning; these will build a lovely deep caramelised flavour. Pour in the wine, then using a wooden spoon, scrape up any sausage bits that have caught on the bottom of the pan.

* Return the vegetables to the pan, then pour in the lentils, including the tin juice. Simmer on low for 4–5 minutes until combined, stir in the spinach until wilted then taste for seasoning. You may want to add salt.

* To make the aioli, combine the egg yolk, mustard, garlic, salt, lemon juice and zest in a large bowl using a balloon whisk. Damp a few sheets of kitchen paper slightly, then place the bowl on the paper to stop it moving about. Drop by drop, pour in the oil while continuously whisking until very thick. This should take a couple of minutes. Don't be tempted to rush pouring in the oil or your aioli will split. Stir in the wild garlic, taste for seasoning then set aside.

——— To assemble

Spoon the lentils onto plates. Dollop over a generous spoonful of the Wild Garlic Aioli, pick over any reserved fennel fronds and wild garlic flowers, then serve immediately.

If your aioli does split, don't worry! Just start with another
egg yolk in a fresh bowl, then very gradually whisk in your
split mixture until nicely combined and thick. The aioli will
keep for 2–3 days in a jar, tightly covered with a lid or cling
film (plastic wrap) in the refrigerator.

2 CARROT AND THYME SAUSAGE BRAISED LENTILS

with Dijon Aioli

SERVES 2 GENEROUSLY (OR 4 WHEN
EATEN WITH BREAD AND/OR SALAD)

1 hour, 15 minutes

4 tablespoons rapeseed (canola),
    vegetable or light olive oil
1 celery stalk, finely sliced on
    an angle
1 onion, peeled and finely sliced
1 large carrot, peeled and finely sliced
    on an angle
a few sprigs of thyme, leaves only
1 teaspoon sea salt flakes, plus extra
    to taste
3 garlic cloves, peeled and finely sliced
4 good-quality pork sausages
200 ml (7 fl oz/scant 1 cup) white wine
1 x 390 g (13¾ oz) tin of green lentils
    in water

Dijon Aioli

1 egg yolk
1½ teaspoons Dijon mustard
½ garlic clove, minced
1 teaspoon sea salt flakes
juice and grated zest of ½ lemon
300 ml (10 fl oz/1¼ cups)
    rapeseed (canola) oil,
    in a jug for easy pouring

SUBSTITUTES

Celery stalk
fennel, leek

Thyme
rosemary

Sausages
minced (ground) pork or chicken

White wine
red wine, water with a splash
of vinegar

* First, heat 3 tablespoons of oil in a large, wide non-stick frying pan (skillet). Add the celery stalk, onion, carrot, thyme, salt and garlic, then fry on medium heat for 10–15 minutes until soft and beginning to turn golden brown.

* Once they're golden and soft, transfer the vegetables to a plate, then increase the heat to high. Next, score each sausage down the middle of its skin and squeeze out the meat into the hot frying pan (discard the skins). Add in 1 tablespoon more oil then fry for 6–8 minutes, using a wooden spoon to crush the meat into rough, large mince. Don't worry about any bits that are catching or burning; these will build a lovely deep caramelised flavour. Pour in the wine, then using a wooden spoon, scrape up any sausage bits that have caught on the bottom of the pan.

* Return the vegetables to the pan, then pour in the lentils, including the tin juice. Simmer on low for 4–5 minutes until combined, then taste for seasoning. You may want to add more salt.

* To make the aioli, combine the egg yolk, mustard, garlic, salt, lemon juice and zest in a large bowl using a balloon whisk. Damp a few sheets of kitchen paper slightly, then place the bowl on the paper to stop it moving about. Drop by drop, pour in the oil while continuously whisking until very thick. This should take a couple of minutes. Don't be tempted to rush pouring in the oil or your aioli will split. Taste for seasoning then set aside.

——— To assemble

Spoon the lentils between plates. Dollop over a generous spoonful of the aioli then serve immediately.

3 FENNEL AND RED WINE SAUSAGE BRAISED LENTILS

with Basil Aioli

SERVES 2 GENEROUSLY (OR 4 WHEN
EATEN WITH BREAD AND/OR SALAD)

1 hour, 15 minutes

4 tablespoons rapeseed (canola),
    vegetable or light olive oil
1 fennel, finely sliced, fronds reserved
1 onion, peeled and finely sliced
1 large carrot, peeled and finely sliced
    on an angle
handful of sage leaves
3 garlic cloves, peeled and
    finely sliced
1 teaspoon sea salt flakes, plus extra
    to taste
4 good-quality pork sausages
200 ml (7 fl oz/scant 1 cup) red wine
1 x 390 g (13¾ oz) tin of green lentils
    in water

Basil Aioli

1 egg yolk
1½ teaspoons Dijon mustard
½ garlic clove, minced
1 teaspoon sea salt flakes
juice and grated zest of ½ lemon
300 ml (10 fl oz/1¼ cups) rapeseed
    (canola) oil
handful of basil leaves, finely
    chopped

SUBSTITUTES

Fennel
leek, celery stalks

Sage
thyme, rosemary, oregano

Sausages
minced (ground) pork or chicken

Red wine
white wine, water with a splash
of vinegar

Basil
spinach and extra lemon zest,
tarragon

* First, heat 3 tablespoons of oil in a large, wide non-stick frying pan (skillet). Add the fennel, onion, carrot, sage, garlic and salt, then fry on medium heat for 10–15 minutes, stirring occasionally, until soft and beginning to turn golden brown.

* Once they're golden and soft, transfer the vegetables to a plate, then increase the heat to high. Next, score each sausage down the middle of its skin and squeeze out the meat into the hot frying pan (discard the skins). Add in 1 tablespoon more oil then fry for 6–8 minutes, using a wooden spoon to crush the meat into rough, large mince. Don't worry about any bits that are catching or burning; these will build a lovely deep caramelised flavour. Pour in the wine, then using a wooden spoon, scrape up any sausage bits that have caught on the bottom of the pan.

* Return the vegetables to the pan, then pour in the lentils, including the tin juice. Simmer on low for 4–5 minutes until combined, then taste for seasoning. You may want to add more salt.

* To make the aioli, combine the egg yolk, mustard, garlic, salt, lemon juice and zest in a large bowl using a balloon whisk. Damp a few sheets of kitchen paper slightly, then place the bowl on the paper to stop it moving about. Drop by drop, pour in the oil while continuously whisking until very thick. This should take a couple of minutes. Don't be tempted to rush pouring in the oil or your aioli will split. Stir in the basil, then taste for seasoning and set aside.

——— To assemble

Spoon the lentils onto plates. Dollop over a generous spoonful of the Basil Aioli, pick over any reserved fennel fronds, then serve immediately.

LENTIL AND MUSHROOM POTSTICKER GYOZAS

45 minutes

2 tablespoons rapeseed (canola) or vegetable oil, plus extra for frying
125 g (4 oz) shiitake mushrooms, finely chopped
1 x 390 g (13¾ oz) tin of green lentils in water, rinsed and drained thoroughly
5 garlic cloves, peeled and minced
thumb-sized piece of fresh ginger root, peeled and finely grated (shredded)
4 spring onions (scallions), finely sliced
2 tablespoons sesame oil
3 tablespoons soy sauce
40 gyoza wrappers (defrosted)

Dipping Sauce

½ teaspoon chilli (hot pepper) flakes
3 tablespoons vinegar (white wine, cider or rice vinegar will work)
4 tablespoons sesame oil
4 teaspoons soy sauce
4 teaspoons sugar (brown or white will work)

SUBSTITUTES

Shitake mushrooms
rehydrated dried wild mushrooms, chestnut mushrooms, portobello mushrooms

Spring onions
leek, red onion

These Japanese dumplings look complicated to make, but I assure you they're really pretty simple. One of my favourite ways to spend a Saturday in London is at my friend Lea's place for gyozas. Lea buys the wrappers from her local Asian grocer and makes up the filling, then we all grab a glass of wine and form a little assembly line for production.

Here I've swapped the more traditional pork mince filling for tinned lentils, meaning vegetarian friends aren't left out. Once made up, the gyoza freeze brilliantly, and it's reassuring knowing they're in the freezer for an almost instant knock-out dinner.

* First, heat the oil in a wide, non-stick pan over a high heat. Add the mushrooms, then fry on high for 4–5 minutes until beginning to catch and any moisture from the mushrooms has evaporated. Transfer to a mixing bowl, then add the lentils, mashing slightly with a fork. Stir in the garlic, ginger, spring onions, sesame oil and soy sauce. Wipe out the pan using kitchen paper.

* Next, set yourself up for gyoza production with a small bowl of water, and a slightly damp tea towel for covering the wrappers (this will prevent them from drying up and cracking). To make a dumpling, add a teaspoonful of the lentil mixture to the middle of a wrapper. Gently dab the edges with water then fold over to create a half-moon shape. Squeeze out any air from the middle, then pleat the edges (see the picture for guidance). Repeat until you've used up all the filling.

* To make the Dipping Sauce, simply stir all the ingredients until combined, then taste for seasoning. You want a nice balance of sharpness from the vinegar, nuttiness from the sesame and saltiness from the soy.

* Cook the gyoza in batches; depending on the size of your pan (you'll need a lid that fits tightly plus a small jug of water), add a few splashes of oil on high heat. Add 6–8 gyozas to the pan and fry for 2–3 minutes until golden on the base. Pour in a few splashes of water, then cover with a lid for 1–2 minutes to allow the gyozas to steam and for the water to fully evaporate. Set aside to a plate, then repeat the process until all the gyozas are cooked. Serve with the Dipping Sauce and eat immediately.

GREEN LENTILS

ROASTED PEPPER, TOMATO AND LENTIL SOUP

with Toasted Almonds

SERVES 4

40 minutes

5 red (bell) peppers
4 tablespoons rapeseed (canola),
     vegetable or light olive oil
2 red onions, finely sliced
3 garlic cloves, peeled and
     finely sliced
2 celery stalks
1 tablespoon butter (salted
     or unsalted)
2 tablespoons paprika
1 teaspoon chilli (hot pepper) flakes
1 x 400 g (14 oz) tin of chopped
     tomatoes
1 x 390 g (13¾ oz) tin of green lentils
     in water
2 tablespoons red wine vinegar
2 teaspoons salt
handful of flaked (slivered) almonds
     (optional)

SUBSTITUTES

Red peppers
yellow or orange (bell) pepper, fresh
ripe tomatoes, sundried tomatoes

Almonds
hazelnuts (filberts), walnuts,
pine nuts

Paprika
cayenne pepper

Red wine
squeeze of lemon juice, any kind
of vinegar, white wine

This soup is inspired by the classic pepper, almond and garlic combination you find in a Spanish romesco sauce, but here I've thrown in some lentils to provide extra heartiness, turning the whole thing into a complete meal.

This recipe is a good one for using up any (bell) peppers that are looking slightly sad and shrivelled in the bottom of the refrigerator. By all means use orange or yellow peppers too if that's what you've got to hand, but I'd avoid green ones as they'll make your soup a bit bitter.

* First, preheat the oven to 210°C (410°F/Gas 8). Roughly chop the peppers, discarding any stalks and seeds, then put them in a roasting tin and toss in 2 tablespoons of oil. Roast for 25 minutes until completely soft and beginning to catch at the edges.

* Meanwhile, heat the remaining 2 tablespoons of oil in a large frying pan (skillet) over a medium heat; add the onions, garlic, celery stalks and butter, reduce the heat to low and gently fry for 10 minutes. Stir in the paprika and chilli flakes, fry for 1–2 minutes until fragrant, then stir in the tomatoes, lentils, including the tin juice, and vinegar. Top up the tomato tin with fresh water and add it to the pan along with the roasted peppers and salt. Bring to the boil and simmer for 5 minutes.

* Using a hand blender, blitz until mostly smooth, leaving some of the lentils whole.

* If serving with the flaked almonds, heat a frying pan on high, add the almonds and toast for 2–3 minutes, stirring regularly to ensure they don't burn, then transfer to a plate.

———— To assemble

Ladle the soup into bowls and scatter over the toasted almonds (if using) to finish.

COOK'S TIP

If you've got a jar of pre-roasted red peppers in your cupboard, you could throw those in the soup instead of roasting fresh peppers. Just make sure you rinse them first to remove any flavour of the brine.

TOMATO BUTTER SUGO

with Fettucine and Feta

Pictured overleaf

SERVES 2

45 minutes

3 tablespoons rapeseed (canola),
    vegetable or light olive oil
3 garlic cloves, peeled and
    finely sliced
1 x 400 g (14 oz) tin of chopped
    tomatoes
¼ teaspoon chilli (hot pepper) flakes
½ onion, peeled (not chopped)
50 g (2 oz) butter (salted or unsalted)
1 teaspoon sea salt flakes, plus extra
    to taste
pinch of sugar (optional)
150 g (5 oz) dried fettuccine
50 g (2 oz) feta

SUBSTITUTES

Onion
half a leek, banana shallot, red onion

Fettuccine
whichever pasta you have to hand

Feta
salted ricotta, Parmesan, halloumi,
pecorino

Chopped tomatoes
passata (sieved tomatoes), peeled
fresh in-season tomatoes

This dish reminds me of Andrew McHarg, an inspiring young chef with a focus on simplicity, and the creative force responsible for transforming my little neighbourhood lunch cafe into Edinburgh's fresh pasta spot by night. It's the first sauce we teach together on our pasta workshop evenings, illustrating how even the simplest of storecupboard ingredients can be turned into something truly comforting and spectacular. Fettucine is my go-to pasta for this rich butter sugo, but by all means, just cook whatever pasta you've got to hand.

* First, heat the oil and garlic in a medium saucepan over a medium heat for 1–2 minutes until fragrant and beginning to golden (take care not to burn the garlic). Add the tomatoes, chilli flakes, onion half, butter and salt. Bring to a simmer, then reduce over a low heat for 25–30 minutes, stirring occasionally. Splash in some water if it's sticking or reducing too much. Remove and discard the onion, then taste the sugo for seasoning. You may want to add a pinch of sugar, depending on the acidity of the tomatoes.

* After 15 minutes of the sugo simmering, bring a large saucepan of water up to the boil and cook the fettucine until al dente (around 9–10 minutes – check packet instructions for exact timing), reserving a mugful of the starchy cooking water. Using tongs, transfer the fettuccine into the tomato sauce, stirring in spoonfuls of the reserved cooking water until coated in the sauce. Taste again for seasoning (bear in mind the feta will add saltiness).

——— To assemble

Divide the pasta between two plates, then finely grate over the feta to finish.

FEAST TIP

Roasted or charred little gem lettuce (bibb lettuce) topped with finely grated (shredded) Parmesan and a squeeze of lemon makes a beautiful side dish to this fettucine (see page 69). Throw in some nice olives, a plate of burrata drizzled with the salsa verde from page 93 plus a good bottle of red and you've got a full-on Italian-style feast.

TOMATOES

TOMATO AND RED WINE BRAISED AUBERGINE

1 hour

200 ml (7 fl oz/scant 1 cup) rapeseed (canola), vegetable or light olive oil (don't be alarmed by the quantity of oil, it's what makes the aubergine skin nicely crisp and smoky)

2 aubergines (eggplants), roughly chopped

2 teaspoons sea salt flakes (as with the oil, don't be alarmed, it won't taste overly salty), plus extra for seasoning

2 onions, peeled and finely sliced

3 garlic cloves, peeled and finely sliced

2 teaspoons ground cumin

2 teaspoons ground coriander

1 x 400 g (14 oz) tin of chopped tomatoes

1 teaspoon chilli (hot pepper) flakes (optional)

400 ml (13 fl oz/generous 1½ cups) red wine

4 tablespoons strained yoghurt (ideally full-fat)

sumac, to serve

handful of dill fronds, lemon zest and crusty bread or flatbreads (all optional)

SUBSTITUTES

Aubergines
courgettes (zucchinis)

Red wine
white wine, water with a splash of vinegar, stock

Onion
spring onions (scallions), leek, shallot

This has become one of our supperclub crowd-pleasers, and while the stage of charring the aubergines (eggplants) does make your kitchen slightly smoky, it's definitely worth opening the windows for! A plate of this braised aubergine is meal-worthy as it is, but serve with some good bread, Whipped Butter Bean Dip (page 83), a few quick pickles and/or Garlic Salted Yoghurt (page 18), and it becomes a full-on celebratory feast.

∗ First, heat the oil in a wide non-stick pan over the highest heat. Carefully, add in half the aubergines, then scatter over the salt. Fry for 8–10 minutes, turning occasionally until charred and blackened. For best results, fry the aubergines in batches so that they fry in a single layer – otherwise they will sweat not fry. Transfer to a plate.

∗ Next, reduce the heat to low, then add the onion and a few splashes of water. Fry for 4–5 minutes, then add the garlic, increase to high then fry for a further 3–4 minutes until soft and translucent. Stir in the cumin and coriander until fragrant. Return the aubergines to the pan, then add the tomatoes, chilli flakes and wine. Simmer for 25–35 minutes until the aubergines are soft and the sauce is reduced. Top up with a few splashes of water at any point if the mixture is catching on the base of the pan. Taste for seasoning; you may want to add more salt.

———— To assemble

Divide the aubergines among four plates, top each with a dollop of yoghurt and the sumac sprinkled on top. Roughly tear over the dill, then zest a little lemon over each to finish (if using). Serve alongside some bread of your choice.

COOK'S TIP

Look for aubergines (eggplants) that are firm and fresh
when buying as these will be tastier and contain less
seeds. If you've got any leftovers of this recipe the next
morning, heat in a frying pan (skillet), then crack in a
few eggs and steam under a lid for a few minutes for
a next-level take on shakshuka.

SPICED LAMB AND TOMATO FLATBREADS

with Mint and Cucumber Yoghurt

25 minutes

2 teaspoons cumin seeds
1 teaspoon fennel seeds (optional)
1 tablespoon rapeseed (canola),
    vegetable or light olive oil
250 g (9 oz) minced (ground) lamb
1 teaspoon sea salt flakes
½ teaspoon ground cinnamon
½ teaspoon chilli (hot pepper) flakes
1 x 400 g (14 oz) tin of chopped
    tomatoes
2 khobez or pitta flatbreads

Mint and Cucumber Yoghurt

½ cucumber, deseeded and finely diced
1 teaspoon dried mint leaves
1 teaspoon sea salt flakes
1 small garlic clove, peeled
    and minced
5 heaped tablespoons strained
    yoghurt (ideally full-fat)

To Serve

handful of mint leaves
1 teaspoon sumac
1 lemon

SUBSTITUTES

Minced lamb
minced (ground) beef, chicken or pork

Cucumber
spring onions (scallions)

Chilli flakes
cayenne pepper, paprika

These are a midweek staple in our house, as I tend to always have some sort of mince stashed away in the freezer. They're inspired by the amazing Turkish eateries I used to go to after work in the Green Lanes area of North London; often family-run restaurants who greet you with plates of warm flatbread, hummus, tzatziki and roughly chopped salad before you've even thought about what you'll order for main.

Here I've used lamb, but of course use minced beef, chicken or pork if that's what is to hand.

* First, add the cumin seeds (and fennel seeds if using) to a large non-stick frying pan (skillet) over a high heat then dry-fry for 1–2 minutes until fragrant. Transfer to a pestle and mortar or cutting board to roughly crush.

* Return the pan to a high heat, then add the oil and the lamb; fry for 3–4 minutes until crispy and gaining some nice dark colour. Stir in the crushed spices, salt, cinnamon and chilli flakes until fragrant. Pour in the tomatoes, then simmer on high for 10 minutes, stirring occasionally until reduced and sticky.

* To make the yoghurt mixture, stir together the cucumber, mint, salt, garlic and yoghurt. Warm the flatbreads in a toaster – or carefully using tongs directly over the gas flame for 20 seconds each side until slightly charred.

——— To assemble

Spoon the mince over a flatbread then add a dollop of the yoghurt. Tear over the mint, a pinch of the sumac, then zest over the lemon to finish.

FENNEL AND LAMB POLPETTE

with Charred Sourdough, Halloumi and Fresh Oregano

SERVES 2

1 hour

4 tablespoons rapeseed (canola),
    vegetable or light olive oil
1 onion, finely diced
1 garlic clove, peeled and minced
2 teaspoons chilli (hot pepper) flakes
1 x 400 g (14 oz) tin of chopped
    tomatoes
1½ teaspoons salt
1 teaspoon caster (superfine) sugar
1½ teaspoons fennel seeds
1 teaspoon ground cumin
250 g (9 oz) minced (ground) lamb
grated zest of 1 lemon
50 g (2 oz) halloumi (optional)
2–3 sprigs of fresh oregano (optional)
2 slices sourdough bread

SUBSTITUTES

Minced lamb
minced (ground) beef, chicken or pork

Halloumi
feta, salted ricotta, pecorino,
Parmesan

Oregano
basil, flat-leaf parsley, mint, dill

Onion
red onion, spring onions (scallions),
leek, shallot

Some of my happiest memories are around the kitchen table at my parents' place in the Scottish Borders; red-wine flowing freely, Buena Vista Social Club's records playing, the smell of my Mum Claire's polpette filling the house as they simmer away in tomato sauce.

I've found halloumi is such a crowd pleasing ingredient, and here it's finely grated raw, offering a natural seasoning to the rich and fragrant polpette. If you're cooking for quite a few people, this recipe is such an easy one to scale up without aded stress.

∗ First, heat the oil in a wide non-stick frying pan (skillet), add the onion then reduce the heat to low and gently fry for 6 minutes, stirring occasionally. Add the garlic and chilli, fry for a further 2 minutes until fragrant then pour in the tomatoes, 1 teaspoon of salt and the sugar. Increase the heat to high, simmer for 10 minutes then, using a fish slice or potato masher, crush the tomatoes to a rough pulp.

∗ Meanwhile, in a second frying pan, toast the fennel seeds on high heat for 1–2 minutes until fragrant. Crush in a pestle and mortar or with a knife, then add to a mixing bowl with ½ teaspoon of salt, cumin, mince and half the lemon zest. Mix to combine the mince then form into roughly 10 meatballs (just under the size of a golf ball).

∗ Next, add quarter of a tin's worth of fresh water to the tomato pulp, followed by the meatballs. Cover with a lid, poach on high for 8 minutes, then remove the lid, gently turn the meatballs and simmer for another 5 minutes or until the meat is cooked in the middle and the sauce is nice and thick. Taste the tomato sauce for seasoning; you may want to add a pinch more sugar or salt, but bear in mind the halloumi will add a sharp saltiness.

∗ Carefully using tongs, char the sourdough over a gas flame for 30 seconds, or until catching at the edges. Or toast it in a regular toaster if you prefer.

——— To assemble

Divide the meatballs between two plates. Using a Microplane zester or fine side of a box grater, grate the halloumi over the top then the remaining lemon zest. Sprinkle the fresh oregano leaves, if using, then serve up with the charred bread.

CHILLED CHILLI TOMATO NOODLES

with Crispy Garlic and Sesame

Pictured overleaf

SERVES 2

25 minutes

3 tablespoons rapeseed (canola), vegetable or light olive oil
5 garlic cloves, peeled and finely sliced
1 x 400 g (14 oz) tin of chopped tomatoes
3 teaspoons miso paste
1 tablespoon cider vinegar
½–1 teaspoon chilli (hot pepper) flakes (depending on how spicy you like things)
4 teaspoons sesame oil
150 g (7 oz) thin wholewheat noodles
2 spring onions (scallions), finely shredded
1 tablespoon toasted sesame seeds

SUBSTITUTES

Cider vinegar
any type of vinegar

Wholewheat noodles
soba, ramen-style or buckwheat noodles

These simple noodles are inspired by afternoons cooking Japanese dishes with food stylist Aya Nishimura. Along with lots of other delicious things, Aya introduced me to the magic of crispy garlic on cold noodles, so I am forever grateful!

If you can, try and get hold of thin soba or wholewheat noodles for this dish, as they're better suited to the delicate, fresh flavours. Chunky egg noodles overpower the miso-tomato sauce slightly, but if that's all you've got, don't worry! You'll still have a delicious meal in front of you.

* First, heat the oil in a frying pan (skillet) on medium, add the garlic and fry for 2–3 minutes until golden (take care not to burn the garlic or it will become overly bitter). Using a slotted spoon, remove the garlic from the pan and transfer to a plate, leaving most of the oil in the pan.

* Next, pour in the tomatoes, miso, vinegar, chilli flakes and sesame oil. Increase the heat to high and simmer for 8–10 minutes until the sauce reduces to a thick concentrate. Using a fish slice or potato masher, mash down to a rough pulp.

* Meanwhile, fill a medium saucepan with water then bring to the boil. Add the noodles then cook until al-dente (around 3–4 minutes – check packet instructions for exact timings). Drain then rinse under plenty of cold water to chill.

* Once the tomato has reduced, taste for seasoning. You want a nice balance of spicy umami from the miso and slightly acidic from the vinegar. Adjust to taste.

——— To assemble

Stir the chilled noodles and tomato sauce in a mixing bowl. Divide between two plates then top with the crispy garlic, spring onions and sesame seeds.

COOK'S TIP

For added meatiness, try frying good-quality bacon lardons until crisp then sprinkle over the noodles.
If you have any leftover miso, try making the caramels on page 144.

TOMATOES

COC
M

SQUASH AND FENUGREEK CURRY

with Ginger and Spinach

SERVES 2 VERY GENEROUSLY
(OR 4 IF EATING
WITH NAAN BREAD)

45 minutes

1 small squash (ideally coquina or
    butternut)
3 tablespoons rapeseed (canola),
    vegetable or light olive oil
1 teaspoon salt, plus extra to taste
2 onions, peeled and finely sliced
4 garlic cloves, peeled and
    roughly crushed
thumb-sized piece of fresh ginger
    root, roughly grated (shredded)
    on the large side of a box grater
1 x 400 ml (14 fl oz) tin of coconut
    milk (ideally full-fat)
2 teaspoons ground turmeric
2 teaspoons ground cumin
1½ teaspoons chilli
    (hot pepper) flakes
1 teaspoon ground fenugreek
grated zest of 1 lemon
1 teaspoon lemon juice
100 g (3½ oz) spinach, washed
    and drained
4 small naan breads

SUBSTITUTES

Squash
cauliflower, (bell) peppers, broccoli

Spinach
chard, kale, shredded savoy cabbage

Ground fenugreek
garam masala, crushed
fenugreek seeds

This recipe will always remind me of Karolina; one of my brilliant founding team members at 27 Elliott's whose face will instantly light up at even the smallest mention of a squash or pumpkin.

Here I've used the spices I tend to have at the back of my cupboard, but I'm sure any Indian-style spices you have to hand will work equally well. Just to keep Karolina happy, this recipe is completely plant-based, making it a good one to have up your sleeve for times when vegan friends come over.

* First, preheat the oven to 190°C (375°F/Gas 5). Roughly chop the squash into large chunks (using a spoon, discard any pips, but don't bother peeling), transfer to a roasting tin then toss in 1 tablespoon of oil and ½ teaspoon of salt. Roast for 25 minutes, tossing halfway through.

* Meanwhile, heat 2 tablespoons of oil in a large, non-stick pan over a medium heat. Add the onion and fry for 5 minutes. Stir in the garlic and ginger, then fry for another 8 minutes until fragrant. Reduce the heat if the garlic looks as though it's going to burn.

* Spoon 3 tablespoons of the white, firm coconut cream at the top of the tin into the onion, then stir in the turmeric, cumin, chilli flakes and fenugreek for 30–60 seconds until fragrant. Pour in the remaining coconut milk from the tin, ½ teaspoon of salt, half the lemon zest and the lemon juice.

* Next, transfer the roasted pumpkin to the sauce, stir in the spinach until wilted then taste for seasoning. You may want to add more salt. Carefully using tongs, char the naan bread on a gas flame for a few seconds until warm and slightly charred (or warm in the oven).

——— To assemble

Divide the curry and naan breads between plates, then zest over the remaining lemon.

COOK'S TIP

If you've got any flaked coconut or almond flakes, gently toast in a dry frying pan (skillet) for 2–3 minutes then sprinkle over before eating.

COCONUT MILK

LIME AND COCONUT PRAWNS

45 minutes

1 x 400 ml (14 fl oz) tin of coconut milk
(ideally full-fat)
½ teaspoon fish sauce
grated zest of 1 lime
½ teaspoon chilli (hot pepper) flakes,
plus extra to garnish
thumb-sized piece of fresh ginger
root, roughly grated on the large
side of a box grater
½ teaspoon turmeric
12 raw king prawns (shrimp), shell-on
stir-fried spinach, to serve (optional)

SUBSTITUTES

Fresh ginger root
lemongrass

Fish sauce
pinch of salt

These prawns (shrimp) are pretty effortless yet feel really special to eat out in the garden on those hot summer nights when you can't be bothered to do much intense chopping and stirring. If you fancied, you could make some steamed jasmine rice or wok greens to serve alongside, but I prefer focusing on the prawns as they are, with a nice glass of white or orange wine, followed by some Salted Coconut Sorbet with Peanuts for pudding (page 65).

My favourite way to serve these is on a big platter with lots of paper napkins and some side plates for the peeled shells and tails. I'm a big believer in the head juices having the most flavour but will leave it up to you if you want to slurp those out or not!

* First, heat a wide frying pan (skillet) over a high heat. Pour in the coconut milk, fish sauce, lime zest, chilli flakes, ginger and turmeric, stirring until combined and rapidly bubbling. Add the prawns and cook for 6 minutes until bright pink, turning halfway through so that they cook evenly. Remove from the heat, then juice in half the zested lime and cut the remaining half into wedges – you can char these in a dry frying pan over a high heat, if you like. Taste the coconut sauce for seasoning; you want a nice balance of coconut sweetness, sourness from the lime, saltiness from the fish sauce and heat from the ginger and chilli.

——— To assemble

Tumble onto a nice serving platter, then top with the lime wedges (plus extra chilli flakes if you fancy) and serve with stir-fried spinach.

COCONUT MILK

COOK'S TIP

If you wanted to remove the prawns' dark digestive tract, use a sharp pair of scissors to cut along the back of each, then pick out the tract and discard.

YELLOW CURRY NOODLE SOUP

with Bean Sprouts and Pickles

25 minutes

1 small onion, peeled and
    roughly chopped
4 garlic cloves, peeled
thumb-sized piece of fresh ginger
    root, peeled and roughly chopped
2 teaspoons dried turmeric
¼ teaspoon chilli (hot pepper) flakes
1 x 400 ml (14 fl oz) tin of coconut milk
    (ideally full-fat)
1 tablespoon rapeseed (canola) oil,
    vegetable or coconut oil
3 teaspoons fish sauce
2 teaspoons lemon or lime juice
1 teaspoon sugar
100 g (3½ oz) rice vermicelli noodles

To Serve

handful of bean sprouts
handful of dill fronds, roughly torn
sprigs of micro red amaranth
    (optional)
2 gherkins (cornichons), finely sliced
4 radishes, finely sliced

SUBSTITUTES

Onion
spring onions (scallions), red onion,
leek

Fresh ginger root
ground ginger

Vermicelli noodles
thin wholewheat noodles, thin egg
noodles, rice

Fish sauce
pinch of salt

This simple supper is inspired by *khanom jeen* – one of my favourite street food lunches from the year I spent studying in Bangkok. I remember the first time I was introduced to these soupy noodles, being amazed to taste dill and cucumber pickles with curry and noodles, flavours I'd always associated more with a Scandinavian style of cooking.

When you buy *khanom jeen* in Bangkok, you're given a big bowl of noodles topped with a soupy fish curry, then you're invited to help yourself to garnishes, usually Hello Kitty-decorated baskets filled with fresh herbs, bean sprouts, and pickles.

In this version, I've kept the sauce pretty quick and simple, but you could fry off some white fish then flake over the noodles too to make the meal even more of a feast. Some shredded grilled (broiled) chicken or crispy tofu would be a nice addition.

* First, put the onion, garlic, ginger, turmeric and chilli flakes in a food processor along with 2 tablespoons of the hard coconut cream from the top of the tin and 3 tablespoons of the thinner coconut milk. Blitz until a smooth paste then add to a medium non-stick saucepan along with the rapeseed oil. Heat on high, stirring the paste regularly in the oil for 2–3 minutes until fragrant and combined. Pour in the remaining coconut milk plus a tin's worth of water, the fish sauce, lemon juice and sugar.

* Meanwhile, boil a full kettle of water. Put the noodles in a large bowl then cover with the boiling water. Allow to sit for 2–3 minutes (check packet instructions for exact timing), or until the noodles are soft, then drain.

* Taste the sauce; you're looking for a nice balance of creamy coconut with salty, sweet, spicy and sour, so add more fish sauce, sugar, chilli flakes or lemon juice to taste if you wish.

———— To assemble

Divide the noodles between two bowls, then pour the soupy sauce over the top. Pile up with bean sprouts, dill, red amaranth, gherkins and radishes, then eat straight away.

CRISPY COCONUT MILK PANCAKES

with Prawns and Garlic Vinegar

Pictured previous

SERVES 2

1 hour

Pancake Batter

200 ml (7 fl oz/scant 1 cup) coconut
  milk (aim for the clear liquid from
  the tin, not the fat)
150 g (5 oz/scant 1 cup) rice flour
½ teaspoon caster (superfine) sugar
½ teaspoon salt (ideally fine salt, but
  sea salt flakes will work too)
¼ teaspoon turmeric
150 g (5 oz) raw prawns (shrimp),
  shelled and deveined, thinly sliced
2 spring onions (scallions), thinly
  sliced, roots discarded
4 tablespoons rapeseed (canola) or
  vegetable oil

Dipping Sauce

2 tablespoons fish sauce
2 tablespoons caster
  (superfine) sugar
2 tablespoons lime juice
2 tablespoons sesame oil
1 garlic clove, peeled and minced
1 small red chilli, finely sliced
  (optional)

To Serve

handful of mint leaves
2 little gem lettuces (bibb lettuces),
  finely shredded
handful of coriander (cilantro) leaves
150 g (5 oz) bean sprouts

My Vietnamese-Californian friend Aimi first introduced me to these
crispy pancakes,; demonstrating just how simple they are to make. If
there's are a few of us eating together, I like to cook up some stir-fried
greens, usually pak choi (bok choi) or Chinese cabbage in oyster sauce
and garlic, plus some steamed jasmine rice. But the pancakes and
dipping sauce alone as-is makesmake a fantastic meal.

* To make the pancake batter, whisk the coconut milk, rice flour, sugar,
salt and turmeric in a large bowl until smooth. If the batter seems too
thick, add in more coconut water or water until you have a pourable batter.
Set aside to sit for half an hour or so (this allows the rice flour to hydrate).

* To make the dipping sauce, stir the ingredients together with
2 tablespoons of warm water until the sugar is dissolved. Taste for
seasoning: you want a nice balance of sweet, salty and sour.

* Next, once the batter has had its time, stir in the sliced prawns and spring
onions. Heat 1 tablespoon of oil in a large non-stick frying pan (skillet),
swirling to ensure an even coverage of oil. Once smoking hot, ladle in
quarter of the batter mix and quickly tilt the pan to ensure an even, thin
layer of batter on the base of the pan. Reduce the heat to medium and
cook for 3 minutes, or until the edges start to brown and the bottom is
crisp and golden (a fish slice or spatula is handy for checking this).

* Carefully flip the pancake and cook on the other side for another
3 minutes then transfer to a plate. Repeat with the oil and batter to
make another three pancakes.

———— To assemble

Layer up two pancakes on each plate with lots of mint, lettuce, coriander
and bean sprouts. Transfer the dipping sauce into a small serving bowl and
eat straight away.

FEAST TIP

These pancakes are really nice to make if you're cooking
for a crowd. I like stir-frying some greens in oyster sauce
to serve alongside: cabbage, pak choi (bok choi) and kale
all work nicely. You could also serve with steamed rice if
you're really hungry.

COCONUT MILK

APPLE, GINGER AND COCONUT BIRCHER MUESLI

SERVES 2

10 minutes, plus overnight soaking

1 x 400 ml (14 fl oz) tin of coconut milk (full-fat or half-fat both work well)
100 g (3½ oz/1 cup) rolled oats
thumb-sized piece of fresh ginger root, finely grated (shredded), tough root discarded
1 crisp eating (dessert) apple, such as Granny Smith, roughly grated (skin-on)
3 tablespoons sunflower seeds, lightly toasted
1 lemon, juiced
yoghurt and honey, to serve (optional)

SUBSTITUTES

Apple
pear, banana

Sunflower seeds
any type of seeds, toasted coconut flakes, nuts

Lemon
lime

There's nothing quite like having a healthy bowl of overnight oats ready to get you feeling smug and organised first thing in the morning. Here, I've included ginger as I feel like it kicks me into action early-on, but with the coconut and oats as your base, have a play with different fruits and spices.

* First, stir together the coconut milk, 200 ml (7 fl oz/scant 1 cup) cold water, rolled oats, ginger, apple, sunflower seeds and a squeeze of the lemon juice. Cover, then pop in the refrigerator to soak overnight.

———— To assemble

Divide the muesli between two bowls then zest over the lemon. Serve with extra yoghurt and honey if you fancy, too.

SALTED COCONUT SORBET

with Peanuts

SERVES 2

5 minutes, plus freezing time

1 x 400 ml (14 fl oz) tin of coconut milk
    (ideally full-fat)
230 g (8 oz/⅔ cup) runny honey
1 tablespoon sea salt flakes
handful of roasted peanuts or handful
    of black sesame seeds (optional)
1 lime

SUBSTITUTES

Runny honey
caster (superfine) sugar, soft
brown sugar

Peanuts
roasted almonds, toasted desiccated
(dried shredded) coconut, pecans

This has got to be one of my favourite puddings in the summer, yet it's almost embarrassingly simple to make. The inspiration is a hybrid of food memories from my travels; the coconut ice cream I'd eat in Bangkok while sat on a tiny plastic stool. There, they serve scoops of it in a small, young coconut, the tender flesh scooped out and scattered over the top. Then, of course, memories of late-night trips to Gelato Messina in Surry Hills, Sydney, where I'd grab their salted coconut ice cream swirled with fresh mango.

* First, blend the coconut milk, honey and salt until combined. Churn in an ice-cream maker, then freeze until you're ready to eat. If you don't have an ice-cream maker, put the mixture in a tupperware tub then, using a fork, break up any ice crystals that form every 30 minutes for 3–4 hours until you have a nice sorbet texture.

———— To assemble

Scoop the sorbet into small bowls or glasses. Roughly crush the peanuts then scatter over. Zest over the lime, then cut into wedges for everyone to squeeze over the juice themselves.

COOK'S TIP

One tablespoon of salt will give you a pretty intense saltiness, which I love, but reduce to ¾ tablespoon if you prefer a more subtle saltiness. If you fancied, you could marinate some chopped mango in the lime juice and zest, then serve that over the top too.

COCONUT MILK

65

ANCH

OVIES

PARMESAN, ANCHOVY AND THYME TOASTS

with Charred Little Gem Lettuce

SERVES 2

15 minutes

2 little gem lettuces (bibb lettuces), bases trimmed and quartered lengthways through the core
3 tablespoons rapeseed (canola) or extra virgin olive oil, plus extra for drizzling
4 sprigs of thyme, leaves only
2 slices of sourdough
1 garlic clove, peeled
1 x 50 g (2 oz) tin of anchovies in olive oil, drained of most of their oil
4 tablespoons Parmesan
1 lemon

SUBSTITUTES

Parmesan
pecorino, salted ricotta, feta

Thyme
chopped rosemary, sage

Little gem
chicory (endive), radicchio

This simple yet beautiful combination is inspired by the dainty anchovy and Parmesan toasts they used to serve at Rawduck in London Fields: just the kind of thing you want to snack on with a good glass of natural wine. Here, I've turned their snack into a complete meal that you can have on the table in just a few minutes – and it's one that will transport you to the Mediterranean sunshine.

I have a growing collection of tinned anchovies in retro packaging from little trips abroad we've made, so when I'm making this at home, I bring the tin to the table along with the grated (shredded) Parmesan, lemon and lettuce, then friends and I can build our own toasts, making the whole meal feel more sociable.

∗ First, lightly coat the little gem quarters in 2 tablespoons of oil. With your gas burner on high, carefully use tongs to hold a few little gem quarters directly over the flame until blistered and charred (take care as it might sizzle and spit slightly). Transfer to a plate and repeat until completed. If you don't have a gas burner, a smoking hot frying pan, griddle pan or hot oven will give the same results – see page 101 for guidance.

∗ Next, heat 1 tablespoon of oil in a small frying pan (skillet) on high. Add the thyme, then fry for 1–2 minutes until crispy and fragrant. Transfer to a plate and set aside.

———— To assemble

Toast the sourdough slices (you could also hold these over a flame for charred, crispy edges). Taking care, rub each slice a few times with the garlic clove, then layer up with the anchovies and fried thyme. Using a Microplane zester or the fine side of a box grater, grate over the Parmesan, then a few zestings of the lemon. Serve with the charred lettuce and a lemon half each for squeezing over juice to taste.

ANCHOVY AND DRIED CHILLI LINGUINE

SERVES 2

20 minutes

200 g (7 oz) dried linguine
5 tablespoons rapeseed (canola)
    or olive oil
1 thick slice of sourdough bread,
    blitzed into breadcrumbs
1 teaspoon sea salt flakes
4 garlic cloves, peeled, crushed and
    roughly sliced
1 x 50 g (2 oz) tin of anchovies in olive
    oil, drained, roughly chopped
1½ tablespoons capers (baby capers),
    drained and roughly crushed
½–1 teaspoon chilli (hot pepper)
    flakes (depending on how hot you
    like things)
5 stems of cavolo nero, de-stalked,
    leaves roughly chopped
zest of 1 lemon

SUBSTITUTES

Cavolo nero
purple broccoli, Brussels sprouts,
kale, savoy cabbage

Linguine
spaghetti, bucatini, farfalle

If capers (baby capers) and anchovies are your thing, this is the ultimate comfort when you can't be bothered to go out and do any shopping for dinner. You can't go wrong with this recipe. All I would say is you don't want to burn garlic when frying or it will become overly bitter. It's worth pretending you're on a cookery show and preparing all the ingredients before you get started, as you want to move quickly once the pasta is cooking!

* First, boil a large saucepan of water, add the pasta and cook until al dente (usually around 7–9 minutes – check packet instructions for exact timings). Reserve a mugful of the starchy cooking water.

* Meanwhile, heat 1 tablespoon of oil in a large non-stick frying pan (skillet) on high, add the breadcrumbs and salt, then fry for 2–3 minutes until golden and crispy. Transfer to a plate then, using a spatula, scrape out the pan and reduce to a medium heat. Add the remaining 4 tablespoons of oil along with the garlic. Fry for 1–2 minutes until beginning to become fragrant and golden, then add the anchovies, capers, chilli flakes and cavolo nero.

* Using tongs, transfer the cooked linguine to the pan with a few splashes of the cooking water. Remove from the heat, then stir until the pasta is nicely coated in the sauce. Splash in more water if it's too dry.

——— To assemble

Divide the linguine between two plates. Top with the breadcrumbs and a good zesting of lemon, then eat immediately.

WARM ANCHOVY DRESSING (*BAGNA CAUDA*)

Pictured overleaf

MAKES ROUGHLY 450 ML
(15 FL OZ/1¾ CUPS), ENOUGH
FOR 6 PEOPLE SHARING

20 minutes

1 x 50 g (2 oz) tin of anchovies in oil
5 garlic cloves, peeled
300 ml (10 fl oz/1¼ cups) milk
    (ideally whole)
400 ml (13 fl oz/generous 1½ cups)
    rapeseed (canola) or olive oil
juice of ½–1 lemon
seasonal vegetables and bread,
    for serving

SUBSTITUTES

Garlic
peeled baby shallots

Lemon
cider vinegar

For minimal effort, this is such a knock-out dip and definitely one to pull together when you've got a crowd to feed. When I'm cooking with friends, I get everyone to help prepare the bits for dunking: raw seasonal veg chopped into crudité-sized pieces, toasted sourdough and some charred baby leeks or purple sprouting broccoli, if it's in season.

* First, in a medium saucepan bring the anchovies (including their oil), garlic and milk to the boil then simmer over a low heat for 10 minutes to infuse. Don't worry if the mixture splits slightly.

* Next, prepare your dipping vegetables by slicing them into crudité-sized pieces.

* Pour the anchovy-infused milk into a food processor and blitz until smooth (you could also use a hand blender). Pour in the lemon juice and then slowly drizzle in the oil; keep blitzing until you've got a thick sauce. Taste for seasoning (you may want to add slightly more lemon juice), then serve while still warm or at room temperature.

COOK'S TIP

The *bagna cauda* will keep in the refrigerator for up to 3 days in a jar or sealed tub so is ideal for prepping ahead of a party. Just allow it to return to room temperature before serving.

ANCHOVIES

SLOW-COOKED ANCHOVY LAMB SHANKS

with Lemony Greens

SERVES 4

30 minutes prep,
plus 3 hours cooking

4 lamb shanks
3 tablespoons rapeseed (canola)
    or light olive oil
1 large or 2 medium onions, peeled
    and finely sliced
2 garlic cloves, peeled and
    roughly crushed
2 tablespoons tomato purée (paste)
3 bay leaves
3 sprigs of rosemary, leaves picked
    and finely chopped
8 anchovies, roughly chopped
500 ml (17 fl oz/2 cups) red wine
500 ml (17 fl oz/2 cups) chicken stock
1 x portion of Frying Pan Flatbreads
    (page 18)
sea salt and freshly ground
    black pepper

Lemony Greens

2 tablespoons extra virgin olive oil
1 garlic clove, peeled and crushed
300 g (10½ oz) cavolo nero, leaves
    roughly torn, stems discarded
juice of 1 lemon ½ teaspoon sea salt
    flakes, plus extra to taste

SUBSTITUTES

Onion
leeks, shallots

Rosemary
thyme

Red wine
dark beer, white wine, cider

Cavolo nero
cabbage, kale, spinach,
rocket (arugula)

This is my idea of a proper Sunday night dinner – ideal for the colder months when comfort food is really needed. For minimal hands-on work and thanks to your oven, you're rewarded with melt-off-the-bone lamb that's beautifully seasoned by the anchovies. Don't worry, they don't make the dish 'fishy' at all, but instead offer a lovely umami hit – just brilliant when served with some lemony greens to cut through all the lamb's fatty richness.

If you wanted to go traditional, some simple roasted potatoes would go nicely with the lamb, but I prefer serving it with the flatbreads from page 18, ideal for mopping up all those lovely slow-cook juices.

* First, preheat your oven to 160°C (320°F/Gas 2). Next, sprinkle the lamb shanks generously all over with lots of sea salt and freshly ground black pepper. Heat a thick-bottomed casserole dish (Dutch oven) (with a lid that fits) over a medium high heat, then pour in 2 tablespoons of oil. Carefully brown the shanks in the dish, taking your time and, if necessary, depending on your dish size, do it in two batches. Once brown all over, transfer to a plate.

* Next, add the onion, garlic, tomato purée, bay leaves and rosemary to the dish, adding the remaining olive oil if the pan looks a little dry. Fry over a medium heat for 10–15 minutes – the steam from the onion will lift off any lamb left on the bottom of the dish from the searing, so stir regularly with a wooden spoon. Once softened and caramelised, stir in the anchovies, using your spoon to break them up and melt them into the onion mixture.

* Increase the heat to high, pour in the red wine and allow to simmer rapidly for 2 minutes, using a wooden spoon to get any sticky Marmite-y bits off the bottom of the dish. Return the lamb shanks to the dish, pour over the chicken stock and bring to a boil.

* Place the lid on the dish and transfer to the oven for 3 hours, removing the lid for the final half an hour of cooking to allow the sauce to reduce and the braised lamb to crisp up a bit at the edges. After 3 hours, the lamb should be tender and falling off the bone.

* Meanwhile, if making the flatbreads, follow the instructions on page 18.

* To make the lemony greens, 15 minutes before serving, heat the oil and garlic in a wide saucepan over a medium-low heat for a minute or so until the oil is fragrant (taking care not to burn the garlic). Add the cavolo nero, toss to combine and cook gently for 8–10 minutes, until wilted down, softened and tender.

* Once the lamb is ready, check the consistency of the sauce. If it is a little loose, transfer the lamb shanks to a covered serving dish to rest and reduce the sauce over a medium heat for 10–15 minutes. Taste for seasoning; you may want to add a bit more salt.

———— To assemble

Toss the cavolo nero with the lemon juice and season to your taste, then transfer to a nice bowl to take to the table. Return the shanks and sauce to the casserole, then serve up at the table, along with the flatbreads for dunking.

PANZANELLA

with Anchovy Dressing

40 minutes

1 yellow and 1 red (bell) pepper,
    halved and deseeded
1 tablespoon rapeseed (canola)
    or light olive oil
½ teaspoon sea salt flakes
1 red onion, peeled, halved and
    finely sliced (a mandolin is
    handy for this)
2 tablespoons red wine vinegar
6 anchovies, roughly chopped
1 garlic clove, peeled and crushed
2 tablespoons extra virgin olive oil
500 g (1 lb 2 oz) mixed, ripe tomatoes
    (preferably in season and an
    assortment of colours and
    shapes), roughly chopped
4 thick slices of slightly stale
    sourdough, crusts removed
    and torn into chunks
1 tablespoon capers (baby capers)
    in brine, drained
small bunch of basil leaves

SUBSTITUTES

Red onion
shallot, white onion

Basil
flat leaf parsley, mint, oregano

Red wine
dark beer, white wine, cider

Cavolo nero
cabbage, kale, spinach,
rocket (arugula)

If you've got any slightly stale bread hanging around, this is a brilliant little tomato and anchovy salad to make, particularly good when you can get your hands on the more interesting varieties of tomatoes throughout the warmer months. Just promise me that you'll keep your tomatoes out of the refrigerator at room temperature – that way they'll have the most flavour and strongest scent.

* First, preheat the oven to 200°C (400°F/Gas 6). Next, in a roasting tin, lightly coat the peppers in rapeseed oil and ¼ teaspoon of salt. Roast for 20 minutes. Once softened and lightly charred all over, remove from the oven and leave to cool. Once cool enough to handle, slice into long strips and set aside.

* Meanwhile, mix the red onion, vinegar and ¼ teaspoon of salt in a large bowl and leave to sit for 5 minutes to lightly pickle.

* Make the anchovy dressing by pounding the anchovies, garlic and extra virgin olive oil together in a pestle and mortar (or roughly chop and stir together in a bowl).

———— To assemble

Add the tomatoes, bread, peppers, capers and half the basil to the onion and toss together to combine. Allow to sit for five minutes so the bread can soak up the flavours. To serve, divide the panzanella between two plates or one giant serving plate. Spoon over the anchovy dressing, and finish by scattering over the individual basil leaves.

ROASTED CHICKEN

with Anchovy and Thyme Aioli and Gem Lettuce

SERVES 4

1 hour, 30 minutes

½ lemon, cut in half (use the other
half for the aioli)
1.5 kg (3 lb 5 oz) free-range chicken
1 garlic bulb, cut in half through the
middle equator
2 tablespoons light olive oil
2 little gem lettuces (bibb lettuces),
quartered into wedges
sea salt and freshly ground
black pepper

Anchovy and Thyme Aioli

1 egg yolk
1 teaspoon Dijon mustard
1 garlic clove, crushed
¼ teaspoon sea salt flakes
juice of ½ lemon
300 ml (10 fl oz/1¼ cups) rapeseed
(canola) oil
8 anchovies in oil, finely chopped
4 sprigs of thyme, leaves picked and
finely chopped

SUBSTITUTES

Whole chicken
chicken legs and thighs (halve the
cooking time)

Little gem lettuce
spinach, rocket (arugula), watercress

This is the way to my heart and it's all about simplicity; garlic and lemon roast chicken that looks after itself in the oven; a big hitting anchovy aioli, and the easiest of greens. I'm far too lazy to be faffing with loads of different trays and oven temperatures for a traditional Sunday roast!

If you fancied potatoes too, I'd recommend par-boiling some waxy, baby potatoes then throwing into the tray with the chicken where they'll soak up all the delicious meat juices and crispy up beautifully.

* First, preheat your oven to 200°C (400°F/Gas 6). Put the lemon half in the cavity of the chicken along with the garlic, then rub the oil all over the chicken skin; season generously with sea salt and freshly ground black pepper. Roast in the oven for 1 hour and 15 minutes. After this time, check the juices run clear by sticking a small knife into the thickest part of the thigh. If still slightly pink, return to the oven for another 10 minutes. You may need to adjust these timings slightly depending on the weight of your bird, so use the packet instructions to guide you. Once the chicken is ready, allow to rest for 10–15 minutes before carving.

* Meanwhile, to make the aioli, combine the egg yolk, mustard, garlic, salt and lemon juice in a large bowl using a balloon whisk. Then, drop by drop, pour in the oil while continuously whisking until very thick (this should take a couple of minutes. Don't be tempted to rush pouring in the oil or your aioli will split). Stir in the anchovies and thyme, then taste for seasoning then set aside.

* Once ready to eat, toss a few spoonfuls of the chicken roasting tin juices together with the lettuce in a large bowl.

——— To assemble

Either pile up the chicken, lettuce and aioli on plates, or transfer everything to the table and allow everyone to help themselves.

Either save the remaining anchovies from the tin in a small sealed container in the refrigerator, then use to make the Parmesan, Anchovy and Thyme Toasts on page 69, or add to the food processor along with 200 g (7 oz) butter (salted or unsalted), then keep in the refrigerator for serving over pan-fried greens, steak or even with some good bread.

If your aioli does split, don't worry! Just start with another egg yolk in a fresh bowl, then very gradually whisk in your split mixture until nicely combined and thick. The aioli will keep for 2–3 days in a jar, tightly covered with a lid or cling film (plastic wrap) in the refrigerator.

BEANS

TARRAGON AND HALLOUMI EGGS

with Crispy Butter Beans and Pickled Tomatoes

20 minutes

1 tablespoon caster (superfine) sugar

2 tablespoons cider vinegar, plus extra to taste

2 handfuls of ripe tomatoes at room temperature, roughly sliced (a mix of colours and shapes is nice if you can get them)

4 tablespoons rapeseed (canola) oil

6 sprigs of tarragon, leaves picked

1½ tablespoons capers (baby capers) in brine, drained

1 x 400 g (14 oz) tin of butter (lima) beans in water, drained

¼ teaspoon salt

4 eggs

50 g (2 oz) halloumi

SUBSTITUTES

Tarragon
sage, rosemary

Halloumi
feta, salted ricotta, Parmesan, pecorino

Cider vinegar
any vinegar

I find tarragon tends to be quite an underrated herb, yet its fresh aniseed quality has the power to transform something very simple and humble, such as a tin of butter (lima) beans. You'll see I've suggested using halloumi in its raw state here; its natural saltiness seasons the eggs and beans perfectly, and gives a nice contrast to the tangy pickled tomatoes. I've designed this recipe with weekend brunch in mind, but if you fancied, it would make a great midweek dinner throughout the warmer months.

* First, stir together the sugar and vinegar in a medium bowl, stir in the tomatoes and set aside while you prepare the rest of the dish, stirring every so often.

* Meanwhile, heat 3 tablespoons of oil in a wide, non-stick frying pan (skillet) over a medium heat. Add the tarragon and capers, then fry for 2–3 minutes until crisp and popped. Carefully using a slotted spoon or fish slice, transfer to a plate, reserving the scented oil in the pan. Take care when frying as there's a chance the capers might spit.

* Next, add the beans and salt to the pan and fry in the oil for 4 minutes until crisp at the edges, stirring occasionally. Using a potato masher or fork, roughly mash one-third of the beans, then stir in half a tin of fresh water until the mixture is nice and creamy. Make four divots in the bean mixture, then splash over the remaining 1 tablespoon of oil. Crack the eggs into the divots, cover with a lid then fry/steam for 4–5 minutes, or until the whites are set and the egg yolk is still runny. Steam for longer if you prefer a firmer yolk.

———— To assemble

Divide the pickled tomatoes between two plates. Top with the eggs and beans, then scatter over the crispy tarragon and capers. Using a Microplane zester or fine side of a grater, finely grate over the halloumi, plus a splash more vinegar to taste.

WHIPPED BUTTER BEAN DIP

with Crispy Herbs

10 minutes

1 x 400 g (14 oz) tin of butter (lima)
    beans in water
2 tablespoons rapeseed (canola) oil
    or vegetable oil, plus 100 ml
    (3½ fl oz/scant ½ cup) for frying
½ teaspoon sea salt flakes, plus
    extra to taste
⅓ clove garlic, peeled and crushed
juice and grated zest of ½ lemon
¾ teaspoon ground cumin
grated zest of ½ lemon, to garnish

Crispy Herbs
selection of any or all of the following:
12 sage leaves
2 sprigs of rosemary, leaves only
2 sprigs of tarragon, de-stalked
2 tablespoons capers (baby capers),
    drained

SUBSTITUTES

Butter beans
cannellini beans, chickpeas
(garbanzos), borlotti beans

Sage leaves
sliced garlic

Rosemary
lemon thyme

This dip is an absolute game-changer; the butter (lima) beans offering an even silkier version of the chickpea-based (garbanzos-based) hummuses I was always used to making. It's how we begin our supperclub evenings at 27 Elliott's, the whipped butter beans spooned onto ceramic dishes and topped with crispy herbs and lemon. I find it incredibly satisfying to peek out from our little kitchen, witnessing strangers connect with each other for the first time as they pass round this dip along with chunks of well-fired sourdough and crisp, raw vegetables from our local growers.

Here I've given the recipe in its simplest form, for dipping into with whichever bread, crisps (chips) or veggies you've got to hand. But I urge you to try it with the Za'atar Roasted Chicken (page 86), or even with some grilled (broiled) fish or charred cauliflower. I suggest taking the step of toasting your cumin before adding it to the beans; as for a minute of extra work, you'll be rewarded with a more intense, deep flavour. Spices that have sat in the back of your cupboard for a while can lose some of their punch, but quickly toasting in a hot pan will bring them fully back to life.

* First, drain the butter beans, reserving 2 tablespoons of the tin juice. Using a food processor or stick blender, blend with the oil, salt, garlic, lemon zest and juice.

* While the processor is still blending, add the cumin to a non-stick pan over a high heat. Toast for 30–60 seconds until fragrant, then add to the processor; continue blitzing until silky smooth. Taste for seasoning and don't be afraid to go heavy on the salt.

* Rinse out and dry the pan, then heat 100 ml (3½ fl oz/scant ½ cup) of oil on high and line a plate with kitchen paper. Carefully add the herbs and capers to the hot oil, fry for 1–2 minutes until crisp then, using a slotted spoon or fish slice, carefully transfer to the paper. If your pan is on the smaller side, I'd recommend frying the herbs in batches.

——— To assemble

Using a spatula or the back of a spoon, spread the dip over a nice plate. Top with the drained crispy herbs and a few splashes of the infused pan oil. Zest over the remaining lemon half to finish.

ZA'ATAR ROASTED CHICKEN AND WHIPPED BUTTER BEAN DIP

with Burnt Greens and Lemon

SERVES 4

45 minutes

4 chicken legs, skin on
1 lemon, cut into rough chunks
1 garlic bulb, cut through the equator
3 tablespoons rapeseed (canola) or olive oil
5 tablespoons za'atar (this is a middle-eastern spice blend; you'll find it in most big supermarkets)
1½ teaspoons sea salt flakes, plus extra to taste
4 little gem lettuces (bibb lettuces), cut into quarters, lengthways
1 x Whipped Butter Bean Dip (page 83)

SUBSTITUTES

Za'atar
sumac, dried oregano, harissa

Little gem
cos (romaine) lettuce, broccolini, kale, cabbage, broccoli

For fairly minimal effort, the elements of this recipe come together beautifully to create a real crowd-pleaser of a feast. I've suggested roasting the gem lettuce as I love tasting how a hot oven or flame can transform even the simplest of leaves, but by all means just serve them raw, dressed in a little fresh lemon juice, oil and salt if that's easier.

* First, preheat the oven to 210°C (410°F/Gas 7). Next, put the chicken, lemon and garlic in a roasting tin. Rub over 2 tablespoons of oil, za'atar and 1 teaspoon of salt, then roast for 25–30 minutes until the skin is dark and crispy and the meat juices run clear when inserted with a knife. Using tongs or a couple of forks, squeeze the roasted lemon juices and caramelised garlic over the chicken.

* In a separate roasting tin, rub 1 tablespoon of oil and ½ teaspoon of salt into the little gem lettuce. Roast for 10–15 minutes until catching at the edges and completely wilted; set aside to cool slightly.

* Meanwhile, make the Whipped Butter Bean Dip by following the instructions on page 83.

———— To assemble

Spoon the dip over the base of four plates. Pile up with the roasted chicken and little gem lettuce, pour over the juices, then eat immediately.

COOKS TIP

It's worth making extra of this recipe then turning it into sandwiches the next day. Just ensure you bring everything back to room temperature before serving to allow all the flavours to come back to life.

THREE WAYS

BRAISED BUTTER BEANS

This is a firm favourite at 27 Elliott's, known to our regulars as 'the beans'. The classic sage and garlic combination is the one dish I've been requested a recipe for the most, yet I'm almost slightly embarrassed when sharing just how simple it is. All I would say is not to rush cooking down the onions, garlic and sage, as it's this fragrant base that makes the dish so special. And whatever you do, don't drain the butter (lima) beans. As you'll find, it's the tin juice that transforms this humble list of ingredients into a rich treat.

If you've got red wine to hand, try making the version with fennel instead. If you've got lots of fresh herbs around, follow the simple steps to make a quick, punchy salsa verde; it goes brilliantly will all three versions and any leftovers will keep well for a few days in the fridge.

Charred sourdough bread is ideal for mopping up the rich bean cooking juices; we toast ours in the cafe directly over a gas flame for a few seconds.

1   SAGE, GARLIC AND WHITE WINE BUTTER BEANS

SERVES 4-6

1 hour

150 ml (5 fl oz/scant ⅔ cup) rapeseed
    (canola) or light olive oil, plus extra
    for finishing
4 onions, peeled and finely sliced
8 garlic cloves, peeled and
    finely sliced
1 large handful of sage leaves (roughly
    5 stalks), leaves picked
2 bay leaves (optional)
3 x 400 g (14 oz) tins of butter (lima)
    beans in water
500 ml (17 fl oz/2 cups) white wine
3 teaspoons sea salt flakes, plus
    extra to taste
grated zest of 2 lemons
    toasted sourdough, to serve
    (optional)

SUBSTITUTES

Sage
oregano, rosemary, thyme

* First, heat the oil over a medium heat in a deep, wide pan. Stir in the onion, garlic, sage leaves and woody stalks and bay leaves, reduce the heat to low and gently sweat for 20–25 minutes, stirring occasionally. You want the onion and garlic to take on a golden colour without burning. If they're catching, add a splash of water to loosen them.

* Add the beans (including the juice from the tin), crushing a handful as you pour them in. Add the wine, salt and enough water to cover, then increase to a rapid boil. Reduce to a simmer for 20–25 minutes then add in most of the lemon zest and taste for seasoning; depending on the acidity of your white wine, you may want to add some lemon juice from your zested lemon. As the beans are quite simple, you may find you need to be quite generous with the seasoning.

* Using a fork, fish out and discard the sage stalks and bay leaves, but you can leave in if you prefer. Crush a few more beans if you'd like a slightly thicker consistency.

——— To assemble

Ladle the beans onto plates, pop a slice of toasted sourdough on each, then generously drizzle over some oil and a bit more lemon zest.

COOK'S TIP

Carefully using tongs, try charring the sourdough oven an open gas flame to give your bread a deep, charred wood-oven flavour.

2   RED WINE AND FENNEL BUTTER BEANS

SERVES 4–6

1 hour

150 ml (5 fl oz/scant ⅔ cup) rapeseed (canola) or light olive oil, plus extra for finishing
2 small fennel, finely sliced (fronds reserved for garnish)
8 garlic cloves, peeled and finely sliced
2 bay leaves (optional)
3 x 400 g (14 oz) tins of butter (lima) beans in water
500 ml (17 fl oz/2 cups) red wine
2 teaspoons sea salt flakes, plus extra to taste
½ teaspoon chilli (hot pepper) flakes (optional)
1 x 400 g (14 oz) tin of chopped tomatoes
toasted sourdough and freshly ground black pepper, to serve (optional)

SUBSTITUTES

Fennel
leek, onion, shallot

Chopped tinned tomatoes
fresh tomatoes, tomato purée

*   First, heat the oil in a deep, wide pan over a medium heat. Stir in the fennel, garlic and bay leaves, reduce the heat to low and gently sweat for 20–25 minutes, stirring occasionally. You want the fennel and garlic to take on a golden colour without burning. If they're catching, add a splash of water to loosen them.

*   Add the beans (including the juice from the tin), crushing a handful as you pour them in. Add the wine, salt, chilli flakes and tomatoes, then increase to a rapid boil. Reduce to a simmer for 20–25 minutes, then taste for seasoning.

——— To assemble

Fish out and discard the bay leaves, if using, ladle the beans onto plates, pop a slice of toasted sourdough on each, then generously drizzle over some oil and plenty of freshly ground black pepper.

3 CAVOLO NERO AND SALSA VERDE BUTTER BEANS

SERVES 4–6

1 hour

150 ml (5 fl oz/scant ⅔ cup) rapeseed
    (canola) or light olive oil, plus extra
    for finishing
4 onions, peeled and finely sliced
8 garlic cloves, peeled and
    finely sliced
2 bay leaves (optional)
3 x 400 g (14 oz) tins of butter (lima)
    beans in water
500 ml (17 fl oz/2 cups) white wine
3 teaspoons salt, plus extra to taste
grated zest of 1 lemon
8 stems of cavolo nero, leaves roughly
    torn, stems discarded
toasted sourdough, to serve (optional)

Salsa Verde

1 small garlic clove
1½ tablespoons capers (baby capers)
    in brine, drained
handful of flat-leaf parsley leaves
handful of basil leaves
2 teaspoons Dijon mustard
200 ml (7 fl oz/scant 1 cup) rapeseed
    (canola) or olive oil
¾ tablespoon cider vinegar
½ teaspoon salt
pinch of sugar (optional)

SUBSTITUTES

Cavolo nero
kale, savoy cabbage, spinach,
wild garlic

Capers
anchovies in oil

Basil/flat-leaf parsley
mint/dill

* First, heat the oil over a medium heat in a deep, wide pan. Stir in the onion, garlic and bay leaves, reduce the heat to low and gently sweat for 20–25 minutes, stirring occasionally. You want the onions and garlic to take on a golden colour without burning. If they're catching, add a splash of water to loosen them.

* Add the beans (including the juice from the tin), crushing a handful as you pour them in. Add the wine, salt and lemon zest, then increase to a rapid boil. Reduce to a simmer for 20–25 minutes, then taste for seasoning.

* Meanwhile, to make the salsa verde, mince the garlic and crush the capers with a knife. Finely chop the flat-leaf parsley and basil, then add the garlic, capers and herbs to a bowl. Stir in the mustard, oil, vinegar and salt, then taste for seasoning. If it's too punchy and vinegary, add a small pinch of sugar.

* In the last few minutes of the beans simmering, throw in the cavolo nero until wilted.

——— To assemble

Fish out and discard the bay leaves, if using, pop a slice of toasted sourdough on each, then generously spoon over the salsa verde.

CHARRED LEEKS, BUTTER BEANS AND CRISPY ROSEMARY

with Goat's Cheese

SERVES 2

20 minutes

3 baby leeks/1 large leek
3 tablespoons rapeseed (canola) or extra virgin olive oil
¼ teaspoon sea salt flakes, plus extra to taste
freshly ground black pepper
a few sprigs of rosemary, leaves only
1 x 400 g (14 oz) tin of butter (lima) beans in water, rinsed and drained
2 tablespoons sherry/red wine vinegar
100 g (3½ oz) soft goat's cheese

SUBSTITUTES

Leek
spring onions (scallions), sweetheart cabbage

Rosemary
sage, tarragon

Goat's cheese
feta, salted ricotta, manchego

Butter beans
chickpeas (garbanzos), cannellini beans

I pop this on our lunchtime menu at 27 Elliott's when the sun comes out in Edinburgh, as the charred leeks hint of BBQ flavours without having to cook outside! Baby leeks are a real treat to use when you can find them as they go incredibly sweet when charred, but a regular leek works brilliantly too. Spring onions (scallions) are a good stand-in for the leeks, so if they are already in the fridge, use those instead!

* First, slice the leek into thick rounds (roughly 2 cm/¾ in thick) and wash well under cold water. If using baby leeks, halve them lengthways. Drain well in a colander then transfer to a mixing bowl along with 1 tablespoon of oil, salt and black pepper, tossing together to coat.

* Next, heat a medium frying pan (skillet) with a lid over a high heat until smoking. Carefully using tongs, add the leeks to the pan cut-side down and fry for 3 minutes, or until charred and blackened on one side. Turn the leeks over and cook for another 2–3 minutes with the lid on; they should be nicely charred and caramelised all over by this point. Transfer the leeks to a plate and cover with the lid where they'll continue to steam and stay warm.

* Return the frying pan to a high heat, splash in 2 tablespoons of oil, then throw in the picked rosemary leaves. Fry for 1 minute, or until the rosemary crisps up, remove from the heat and set aside.

* Put the drained butter beans and charred leeks in a bowl, then stir in the vinegar and crispy rosemary leaves (but not the pan oil). Season to taste – you may want to add more salt.

——— To assemble

Divide the dressed beans between two plates. Crumble over nuggets of the cheese, then spoon over the rosemary-infused pan oil to finish.

SWEE

CORN

CORNBREAD LOAF

with Cumin and Chilli Butter

45 minutes

350 ml (12 fl oz/1½ cups) milk
4 eggs
60 ml (2 fl oz/¼ cup) rapeseed
    (canola) or olive oil
5 spring onions (scallions), finely
    shredded, roots discarded
1 x 340 g (11½ oz) tin of sweetcorn,
    drained
200 g (7 oz/1⅔ cups) plain
    (all-purpose) flour
1 teaspoon baking powder
1 teaspoon caster (superfine) sugar
    or soft brown sugar
2 teaspoons sea salt flakes
handful of coriander (cilantro) leaves

Cumin and Chilli Butter

1 tablespoon ground cumin
125 g (4 oz) butter (salted or unsalted)
juice and grated zest of 1 lime
1 teaspoon sea salt flakes
1 teaspoon chilli (hot pepper) flakes,
    plus more to taste

SUBSTITUTES

Cumin
paprika

Baking powder
bicarbonate of soda

Lime
lemon

This loaf is inspired by the polenta-based (cornmeal-based) cornbread they serve at Caravan in King's Cross; my go-to lunch spot after a train ride down to London from Edinburgh. I've simplified things slightly, using plain (all-purpose) flour from the back of the cupboard instead of polenta.

* First, preheat the oven to 200°C (400°F/Gas 6), then line a large loaf tin with baking parchment widthways, an 18 cm x 9 cm (7 in x 4 in) tin works nicely.

* Next, whisk together the milk, eggs, oil and spring onions in a large bowl. In another mixing bowl, stir together the sweetcorn, flour, baking powder, sugar and salt, then stir in the egg mixture until combined to a batter. Pour into the loaf tin and bake for 35 minutes, or until golden brown.

* To make the cumin and chilli butter, heat the cumin in a frying pan (skillet) for 1–2 minutes on medium until fragrant (take care not to burn it). Transfer to a food processor along with the butter, lime zest and juice, salt and chilli flakes. Blitz for 3–4 minutes, or until really soft and whipped, then taste for seasoning. You may want to add more salt or chilli.

* Allow the loaf to cool for 5 minutes in the tin, then turn out and cut into 8 slices.

——— To assemble

Divide the slices of cornbread among plates, spread over plenty of butter then tear over the coriander to finish.

FEAST TIP

To make this into a larger brunch, griddle or grill (broil) the cornbread slices, then layer up with fried eggs, sliced avocado, ripe tomatoes and finely sliced chilli.

COOK'S TIP

Don't worry if you don't have a loaf tin. Just grease a muffin or cupcake tray with rapeseed (canola) or vegetable oil, then make individual muffins.

SWEETCORN FRITTERS AND CHARRED LITTLE GEM LETTUCE

Pictured overleaf

with Basil Aioli

SERVES 2 GENEROUSLY
(MAKES 8 FRITTERS)

40 minutes

1 x 340 g (12 oz) tin of sweetcorn
   in water, drained
6 spring onions (scallions),
   finely sliced on an angle
3 tablespoons plain
   (all-purpose) flour
2 eggs
½ teaspoon sea salt flakes,
   plus extra to sprinkle
150 ml (5 fl oz/scant ⅔ cup) rapeseed
   (canola) or vegetable oil for frying
1 little gem lettuce (bibb lettuce), cut
   into quarters through the core

Basil Aioli

1 egg yolk
1½ teaspoons Dijon mustard
½ garlic clove, peeled and minced
1 teaspoon sea salt flakes
juice and grated zest of ½ lemon
300 ml (10 fl oz/1¼ cups) rapeseed
   (canola) oil
handful of basil leaves,
   finely chopped

SUBSTITUTES

Spring onion (scallion)
red onion

Baby gem lettuce
baby leeks, spring onions (scallions)

Lemon
lime

Basil
flat leaf parsley, tarragon leaves

These are a staff lunch favourite at 27 Elliott's and always remind me of the brunch spots I'd spend time in when living in Sydney. I'm often asked what the key to good fritters is, and my response is always a good non-stick pan, plus the bravery to let the fritters do their thing when frying and not interfere too much, as this is what causes them to break up!

Here I've teamed the fritters with a fresh herby aioli and some charred little gem lettuce (bibb lettuce), turning them into a complete meal, but if you fancied a lighter snack or starter, the fritters as they are with a wedge of lemon for squeezing over are a beautiful thing too!

∗ First, stir together the drained sweetcorn, spring onions, flour, eggs and salt in a large mixing bowl, then set aside to rest.

∗ To make the aioli, combine the egg yolk, mustard, garlic, salt and lemon juice/zest in a large bowl using a balloon whisk. Damp a few sheets of kitchen paper slightly, then place the bowl on the paper to stop it moving about. Then, drop by drop, pour in the oil while continuously whisking until very thick. This should take a couple of minutes. Don't be tempted to rush pouring in the oil or your aioli will split. Stir in the basil, then taste for seasoning. Transfer to a small serving bowl, then set aside.

∗ Heat a wide, non-stick frying pan (skillet) over a high heat, then pour in enough oil to thinly coat the surface. Using tongs, fry the little gem lettuce in a single layer for 3 minutes on each side, or until the wedges are charred and wilted. Transfer to a plate.

∗ Next, pour another layer of oil into the hot pan, then line a plate with a few sheets of kitchen paper. After a minute or two, test the oil is hot enough for frying the fritters by adding a pinch of the mixture to the pan. If it sizzles and bubbles, you're ready for frying. Gently spoon the mixture into the pan, taking care not to overcrowd the pan. Allow the fritters to cook on one side for 3–4 minutes, then carefully using a fish slice or spatula, flip and fry for another 3–4 minutes. Try not to move the fritters around too much as this will ensure they don't break up. Transfer them to the lined paper and sprinkle with salt. Repeat to use all the mixture.

——— To assemble

Divide the fritters between two large plates. Add the charred lettuce, then finish with a generous dollop of basil aioli.

CHARRED SWEETCORN AND CUMIN SEED TACOS

with Pickled Red Cabbage and Feta Mayonnaise

30 minutes

½ small red cabbage, finely sliced, white core discarded
2 teaspoons salt
4 tablespoons cider, white wine or red wine vinegar
3 tablespoons sugar, ideally caster (superfine)
2½ teaspoons cumin seeds
3 tablespoons rapeseed (canola), vegetable or light olive oil
1 x 340 g (12 oz) tin of sweetcorn in water, drained
2 spring onions (scallions), finely sliced on an angle
1 teaspoon ancho chilli (hot pepper) flakes or ½ teaspoon regular chilli flakes
1 avocado
juice of ½ lime
100 g (3½ oz) feta
2 tablespoons mayonnaise (or plain yoghurt)
4 small or 2 big wraps (corn or wheat)
chilli sauce (optional)

SUBSTITUTES

Red cabbage
white cabbage, carrots, radishes

Feta
goat's cheese, mature Cheddar

Cumin seeds
coriander seeds

When I'm cooking at home with friends, I've found everyone likes to be given a job to contribute to the meal. This recipe is ideal for those occasions and, with simple delegation, means you've got a lovely little taco feast ready in just a few minutes. I've given you quantities for two people, but just scale up depending on how many of you are eating.

Don't be scared to let your sweetcorn burn and blister here, as that's what gives the kernels such a beautiful, smoky flavour. I promise it's worth opening the windows for!

* First, stir together the cabbage, 1 teaspoon of salt, vinegar and sugar, ensuring each piece of the cabbage is fully coated, then set aside for 15 minutes to quickly pickle.

* Next, toast the cumin seeds in a wide frying pan (skillet) over a high heat for 1–2 minutes until fragrant, then transfer to a cutting board and lightly crush (or crush in your pestle and mortar if you have one). Return the pan to a high heat, then pour in the oil, drained sweetcorn and 1 teaspoon of salt. Fry the sweetcorn for 6–7 minutes until charred and black at the edges. Add the spring onions, chilli flakes and half the crushed cumin, then stir together over a medium heat for 1 minute.

* Meanwhile, halve the avocado, carefully remove the stone and scoop spoonfuls of the flesh into a small bowl; stir in the lime juice. In another small bowl, crush the feta and stir in the mayonnaise.

* Warm the wraps in a dry frying pan or, using tongs, directly over the flame of your gas hob for a few seconds (take extra care!) until slightly charred in some spots.

——— To assemble

Take the wraps, pan of sweetcorn, cabbage pickles, avocado and feta-mayonnaise to the table. Transfer the remaining cumin seeds to a small dish. Allow everyone to build their own tacos, adding extra chilli sauce, to taste, if you like things hot!

INDIAN-STYLE CREAMED CORN

with Naan, Coriander and Toasted Spices

SERVES 2

25 minutes

6 tablespoons rapeseed (canola),
    light olive or coconut oil
1 onion, peeled and finely sliced
3 garlic cloves, peeled and finely sliced
2 x 340 g (11½ oz) tins of sweetcorn,
    drained
2 teaspoons ground coriander
1½ teaspoons ground cumin
1 tablespoon curry leaves (optional)
½–1 teaspoon of dried chilli (hot
    pepper) flakes (depending on
    how spicy you want it)
1 lemon
sea salt flakes
1 large naan or 2 chapatis
handful of coriander (cilantro) leaves

SUBSTITUTES

Onion
leek

Ground coriander
garam masala

Lemon
lime

This is half way between a dahl and a curry, where a few tins of regular sweetcorn are transformed into something fragrant and special by the help of the spices from the back of your cupboard.

I've suggested using a stick blender to give your corn a nice creamy texture, but if you don't have one, don't worry, just mash some of the corn by hand using a potato masher instead.

* First, heat 4 tablespoons of oil over a medium heat in a wide pan. Add the onion and garlic, reduce to low, then fry for 15 minutes until soft and translucent. Stir occasionally and add a splash of water if beginning to catch.

* Add half the corn to a jug with a splash of water. Then, using a stick blender or food processor, blitz into a rough pulp.

* Add 2 tablespoons of oil to the onion, then add the spices and curry leaves. Stir for 1–2 minutes until fragrant, then add the creamed corn and reserved kernels. Add the zest of one lemon and the juice of half, plenty of seasoning to taste, and a splash of water to loosen if it's too thick. Cut the remaining lemon half into wedges.

* Meanwhile, use tongs to heat the naan bread directly over a gas flame for a few seconds until lightly charred. You can also do this in a hot pan or oven.

——— To assemble

Divide the corn and naan between two plates. Roughly tear over the coriander and serve with a lemon wedge each.

CHIC

PEAS

TURMERIC CHICKPEAS

with Garlic Yoghurt and Shaved Radish

<u>SERVES 2</u>

30 minutes

1½ teaspoons cumin seeds
1 teaspoon fennel seeds
3 tablespoons rapeseed (canola),
    light olive or vegetable oil
1 onion, peeled and finely sliced
3 garlic cloves, peeled and sliced
1½ teaspoons mustard seeds
1 teaspoon ground turmeric
½–1 teaspoon chilli (hot pepper) flakes
1 x 400 g (14 oz) tin of chickpeas
    (garbanzos) in water, (don't drain
    it – you want the tin juice)
1 teaspoon sea salt flakes,
    plus extra to taste
juice and grated zest of ½ lemon,
    plus 1 lemon, halved, to serve
4 radishes
Garlic Salted Yoghurt (page 18),
    to serve

SUBSTITUTES

Cumin/fennel seeds
coriander seeds, fenugreek seeds

Chickpeas
butter (lima) beans

Radishes
cucumber

These curried chickpeas (garbanzos) appear on the cafe lunch menu at the start of the year, offering some colour and spice to contrast with winter's dark afternoons. Here, I've used cumin, fennel and mustard seeds as the standout spices, but have a play with the spices you've already got in the cupboard.

* First, add the cumin seeds and fennel seeds to a large frying pan (skillet) over a high heat and toast for 1–2 minutes until fragrant, then transfer to a plate and set aside.

* Next, reduce the heat to medium, add the oil, onion, garlic and mustard seeds; fry for 15–20 minutes, stirring regularly until soft. Stir in the turmeric, toasted cumin and fennel seeds, and chilli flakes for 1 minute, then pour in the chickpeas, including the tin juice, salt, lemon juice and zest. Simmer for 10 minutes until thickened, then season to taste. If it's reducing too quickly and catching on the bottom of the pan, throw in a few splashes of water.

* Finely slice the radish and sit in a bowl of cold water (a mandolin is really handy for this!). To give a little boost of flavour, you can fry the lemon halves, cut-side down, in a frying pan over a high heat, until charred.

———— To assemble

Divide the chickpeas between two plates. Dollop over the yoghurt then top with the radish and serve with lemon wedges.

COOK'S TIP

If you fancied, you could pickle the radish in a few splashes of vinegar, a pinch of salt and some sugar. This will make the radish turn super-bright pink and add a nice tang to the chickpeas. The Frying Pan Flatbreads (page 18) are also delicious alongside.

THREE WAYS

BROWN SUGAR CHICKPEA MERINGUE

As well as being brilliant for thickening braises, such as the one on page 110, chickpea (garbanzo) water, (also known as aquafaba) acts as a fantastic stand-in for eggs when making meringues – the type with a crunchy outside and chewy middle. You'll notice in these meringues I use more dark brown sugar than white caster (superfine) sugar. This is because I love the deep molasses vibe it brings.

This is such a good recipe to have up your sleeve, especially for any vegan friends coming round for dinner. Just a heads-up: unless you have super-powered biceps, you will need a hand-held blender or food processor with whisk attachment as it takes a few more minutes to whip the chickpea water into cloudy peaks than it does with egg whites.

BROWN SUGAR CHICKPEA MERINGUES

MAKES 8 MEDIUM MERINGUES

30 minutes, plus baking time

150 ml (5 fl oz) chickpea (garbanzo)
    juice, drained from 1 x 400 g (14 oz)
    tin of chickpeas in water (use the
    chickpeas for the shaved fennel
    salad on page 120)
1 teaspoon sea salt flakes
1 teaspoon lemon juice
50 g (2 oz/¼ cup) caster
    (superfine) sugar
100 g (3½ oz/½ cup) dark brown sugar

* First, preheat the oven to 120°C (250°F/Gas 1), then line two large baking trays (pans) with baking parchment.

* Next, whisk the chickpea juice, salt and lemon juice in a large mixing bowl until you've got very stiff peaks; this will take around 5 minutes. Combine the sugars, then whisk 1 tablespoon of the sugar mix into the chickpea juice, ensuring it's fully dissolved and not grainy. You can check the mixture is smooth and not grainy by rubbing a small amount between two fingers. Repeat until all the sugar has been integrated and the mixture is smooth and glossy.

* Dot some of the mixture between the baking paper and the tray to help it stick down, then spoon eight large mounds across the two trays and bake for 2 hours. Try not to open the oven door to prevent the meringues collapsing, then allow to cool completely before serving.

COOK'S TIP

Stored in an airtight container, the meringues will keep for up to 4 days. If you don't have a very powerful electric whisk, add 1 teaspoon cream of tartar to the chickpea juice before whisking; this will help it hold its shape.

1 COCOA AND COFFEE CREAM

300 ml (10 fl oz/1¼ cups) double
   (heavy) cream
4 shots of espresso, cooled
2 tablespoons runny honey
4 tablespoons cocoa (unsweetened
   chocolate) powder

Using a hand-held blender, whip the cream until soft peaks (take care not to over-whisk or the cream will become grainy). Fold in the espresso and honey, continue whisking to thicken, then spoon over the meringues, followed by a dusting of sieved cocoa.

2 ORANGE, YOGHURT AND TAHINI

2 oranges (blood oranges are nice
   when they're in-season)
200 g (10½ oz/1¼ cups) strained
   yoghurt
4 tablespoons tahini (stirred in the
   jar if the oil has separated)

First, slice the top and bottom off the oranges, then carefully cut away the peel and white pith. Cut out the fleshy segments and transfer to a bowl. Spoon the yoghurt over the meringues, add a few segments of orange then, using a clean spoon, swirl over the tahini and eat immediately.

3 POACHED RHUBARB

2 sticks of rhubarb, ends trimmed,
   cut into 3 cm (1 in) lengths
5 tablespoons caster (superfine)
   sugar
juice and zest of 1 orange
   (zest peeled with a speed
   peeler into rough strips)

Put the rhubarb, sugar, orange zest and juice in a large, wide pan. Top up with 100 ml (3½ fl oz/scant ½ cup) water, then heat on high heat for 6–8 minutes, or until the rhubarb is soft but still keeping its shape and the juice thickens to a syrup. Remove from the heat, set aside and allow to cool before spooning over the meringues.

CHICKPEA AND SPINACH DOSAS

with Quick Mango Salsa

SERVES 4

1 hour

2 medium sweet potatoes, peeled
   and roughly diced into 2 cm
   (¾ in) cubes
1 tablespoon rapeseed (canola) or
   light olive oil
2 tablespoons coconut oil (or use
   light olive or rapeseed (canola)
   oil if you don't have coconut)
1 onion, peeled and finely sliced
1 garlic clove, peeled and crushed
1 tablespoon black mustard seeds
1 tablespoon good quality curry powder
1 x 400 g (14 oz) tin of chickpeas
   (garbanzos) in water (don't
   bother draining)
300 g (10½ oz) spinach, washed
1 teaspoon sea salt flakes,
   plus extra to taste

Mango Salsa

1 large mango, peeled and diced
½ red onion, peeled and finely sliced
   (a mandolin is handy for this)
1 small red chilli, finely chopped
   (optional)
small bunch of coriander (cilantro)
   leaves, finely chopped
juice and grated zest of 1 large lime
   (use 2 limes if yours are small and
   not so juicy)
¼ teaspoon sea salt flakes

Dosa Batter

100 g (3½ oz/¾ cup) chickpea
   (gram) flour
100 g (3½ oz/¾ cup) plain
   (all-purpose) flour
½ teaspoon bicarbonate
   of soda (baking soda)
¼ teaspoon sea salt
4 tablespoons rapeseed (canola)
   or light olive oil

This might look like quite a few ingredients to gather for one meal, but I'm hoping you have most of them in your cupboard and refrigerator already. You'll increasingly find chickpea (gram) flour in the larger supermarkets, and once you've got into the swing of making these dosas, you can use the flour to knock up a quick batter and fill with whichever veggies you've got that need using up, or to serve alongside the dahls on pages 18–21. If making your own mango salsa is one step too far, just grab some good-quality mango chutney from a jar instead.

* First, preheat your oven to 200°C (400°F/Gas 6). Next, mix the sweet potato and oil in a roasting tin, then roast for 25 minutes, until golden brown all over and soft to touch when pressed with a fork.

* Meanwhile, heat the coconut oil in a wide frying pan (skillet) over a medium heat. Add the onion, garlic, mustard seeds and curry powder, then gently fry for 10 minutes until soft and caramelised.

* Pour in the chickpeas, including their tin water, then simmer for 5 minutes or so until thickened and creamy. Reduce the heat to low, then stir in the spinach and salt to wilt it. Splash in a tablespoon of water if the mixture looks too dry.

* When the sweet potatoes are ready, add to the pan and lightly crush with a potato masher or fork, until roughly combined. Remove from the heat, taste for seasoning – you may want to add more salt – then set aside.

* To make the mango salsa, simply mix all the ingredients together in a medium bowl and taste for seasoning. It should be sharp, fresh and punchy.

* Make the dosa batter by whisking all the ingredients together, except for the oil, with 400 ml (13 fl oz/generous 1½ cups) warm water. Next, heat 1 tablespoon of oil in a wide, non-stick frying pan, swirling to ensure an even coverage in the pan. Once smoking hot, ladle in a quarter of the batter mix and quickly tilt the pan to ensure an even, thin layer of batter on the base of the pan (as if you were making a crepe). Reduce the heat to medium and cook for 1 minute, or until there are bubbles appearing all over and the bottom is crisp and golden. Using a spatula, carefully flip, then cook for a further minute. Transfer to a plate. Repeat with the oil and batter until you've got four pancakes.

Sweet potatoes
pumpkin, carrots

Onion
leek

Spinach
chard, peas, cabbage

——— To assemble

Take the plate of dosa pancakes to the table, along with the chickpea mixture and the salsa. Allow everyone to pile and roll up their own wraps.

SHAVED FENNEL, SUMAC ONIONS AND CHICKPEA SALAD

with Toasted Almonds

SERVES 2

40 minutes

1 small red onion, peeled, halved and finely sliced
1 tablespoon sumac
1 tablespoon red wine vinegar
½ teaspoon sea salt, plus extra to taste
1 fennel, tough outer layers removed, trimmed (fronds reserved for garnish)
70 g (2¼ oz/½ cup) whole blanched almonds
1 x 400 g (14 oz) tin of chickpeas (garbanzos) in water, drained
1 large handful of flat-leaf parsley leaves, roughly chopped
juice of ½ lemon
2 tablespoons extra virgin olive or rapeseed (canola) oil
freshly ground black pepper

Here I've used sumac (the crushed Middle-Eastern berry) to add a lemony hit to finely sliced red onion, forming a quick pickle that lifts a regular tin of chickpeas (garbanzos) into a bright and satisfying salad. If you can't find sumac, just finely grate in some lemon zest instead. This simple assembly of ingredients is particularly good for eating in the sunshine with a glass of cold white wine.

* First, preheat the oven to 180°C (350°F/Gas 4). Next, mix the sliced red onion in a bowl with half of the sumac, the vinegar, and ¼ teaspoon of salt. Massage well and set aside to soften for 10 minutes.

* Meanwhile, using a sharp knife (or a mandolin if you have one), thinly shave the fennel. Put it in a bowl of cold water while you prepare the rest of the ingredients; this will keep it fresh and crisp.

* Toast the almonds on a baking (cookie) sheet for 8–10 minutes, until golden and fragrant. Once cool enough to handle, roughly crush and chop.

* Drain and dry the fennel well using kitchen paper or a clean tea towel. Mix with the chickpeas, sumac onions, flat-leaf parsley and reserved fennel fronds in a large bowl. Dress with the lemon juice, oil, ¼ teaspoon salt and freshly ground black pepper, then toss well to combine.

———— To assemble

Divide between two plates and serve with a scattering of the toasted almonds and the remaining sumac sprinkled on top.

FEAST IDEAS

Grilled (broiled) or barbecued fish is ideal for turning this salad into more of a celebratory feast. My favourite is fresh mackerel rubbed in oil then charred over coals. If you fancied, some griddled king prawns (shrimps) would work well with the salad too, as would your favourite cut of steak.

CAULIFLOWER, SWEET POTATO AND CHICKPEA TRAYBAKE

with Coriander Sambal

SERVES 4

55 minutes

2 tablespoons coconut, rapeseed
  (canola) or vegetable oil
2 tablespoons mustard seeds
1 x 400 ml (14 fl oz) tin of coconut milk
  (ideally full-fat)
thumb-sized piece of fresh ginger
  root, peeled and finely grated
  (shredded)
3 garlic cloves, peeled and crushed
2 teaspoons ground cumin
1½ teaspoons ground turmeric
1 teaspoon sea salt flakes,
  plus extra to taste
1 large cauliflower, outer leaves
  removed, cut into wedges
  through the stem
2 sweet potatoes, cut into wedges,
  (don't bother peeling the skin)
100 g (3½ oz) spinach, washed
1 x 400 g (14 oz) tin of chickpeas
  (garbanzos) in water, rinsed
  and drained
chapatis (optional), to serve

Coconut and Coriander Sambal

3 tablespoons coconut chips/
  dried shavings
handful of coriander (cilantro) leaves
1 green chilli, deseeded
juice and grated zest of 1 lime
¼ teaspoon sea salt flakes

The brilliant thing about this recipe is that your oven does all the hard work to make a flavour-packed curry; freeing you to blitz up a bright and zingy sambal. Here I've suggested using coconut chips to mix with the coriander (cilantro) and lime, but use any toasted nuts or seeds that you've got to hand.

* First, preheat the oven to 200°C (400°F/Gas 6). Melt the coconut oil in a large, deep tray on the stove over a high heat, then add the mustard seeds and fry for 1–2 minutes, or until they begin to pop. If your stove isn't gas, this can be done in a frying pan (skillet) then transferred to the tray, or even done in the oven. Stir in the coconut milk, ginger, garlic, cumin, turmeric, salt, cauliflower and sweet potato. Transfer to the oven and roast for 40 minutes, stirring halfway through.

* To make the sambal, blitz together the coconut chips, coriander (stalks and leaves), chilli, lime zest and juice, and salt with a few splashes of water in a food processor, until you get a rough texture. You can also do this by chopping and mixing everything by hand.

* Remove the tray from the oven and set aside the cauliflower and sweet potato to make space for the spinach and chickpeas. Stir until the spinach is wilted, adding a splash of water if it's a bit dry. Heat the chapatis in a warm oven or, carefully using tongs, hold over the gas flame on your cooker for a few seconds.

———— To assemble

Divide the curried chickpeas among four plates, top with the roasted cauliflower and sweet potato, then spoon over the sambal. Serve with the chapatis on the side for mopping up the spiced roasting juices.

Coconut flakes
toasted almonds, pumpkin seeds,
cashews, sunflower seeds

Sweet potato
carrot, pumpkin

Chickpeas
butter beans, cannellini beans

ALMOND CHERRY FRIANDS

MAKES 10 FRIANDS

40 minutes,
plus 20 minutes cooling time

180 g (6 oz) butter (salted or unsalted)
50 g (2 oz/scant ½ cup) plain
  (all-purpose) flour
180 g (6 oz/1½ cups) icing
  (confectioner's) sugar
100 g (3½ oz/1 cup) ground almonds
grated zest of 2 lemons
5 egg whites
pinch of salt
1 x 400 g (14 oz) tin of pitted cherries,
  drained and juice squeezed out
  (save the syrup to make the Cherry
  and Tarragon Soda on page 138)

SUBSTITUTES

Ground almonds
ground hazelnuts, ground pistachios

Butter
vegetable oil

These dainty little almond-based cakes are brilliant with an afternoon coffee and are really easy to pull together. Here, a trusty tin of cherries is the hero, but use fresh strawberries, raspberries or blackberries when they're in-season if you fancy too.

Traditionally, friands are made in their own oval-shaped moulds, but I just stick with a regular cupcake tray as I like to keep kitchen kit pretty minimal. If you wanted, you could also line the tin with muffin or cupcake cases, making them easier to transport if you're taking them round to a friend's place.

∗ First, preheat your oven to 180°C (350°F/Gas 4). Heat the butter in a small saucepan over a medium-high heat for 5–7 minutes. Watch it carefully and keep on the heat until it becomes a dark, nutty, golden colour. Allow to cool slightly, then using a pastry brush, grease 10 of the moulds in a cupcake baking tray (pan) or friand tray if you have one. Alternatively, line with 10 paper cupcake/muffin cases.

∗ Meanwhile, stir the flour and sugar (sieve your icing sugar if it's lumpy) in a large mixing bowl, then add the ground almonds and lemon zest. In a separate bowl, beat the egg whites to a soft, light foam using a whisk, then pour into the flour mix along with the melted butter. Mix lightly but thoroughly, then pour into the buttered moulds. Pop three cherries into each mould, then bake for 15–20 minutes.

∗ Remove from the oven, then leave to settle for 20 minutes before carefully removing from the trays with a knife.

COOK'S TIP

This is a really versatile friand mixture that lends itself to all kinds of soft fruit, so have a play with whichever berries you have to hand. If using frozen, though, just ensure they're really well-drained, as too much juice will make your friends soggy.

DARK CHOCOLATE MOUSSE

with Pickled Cherries

SERVES 6

30 minutes,
plus 2 hours chilling time

55 g (2 oz) whole blanched hazelnuts
    (filberts)
150 g (5 oz) chocolate with at least 70%
    cocoa solids, broken into chunks
2 tablespoons butter
    (salted or unsalted)
3 yolks and 5 egg whites (keep the
    spare yolks for making aioli on
    pages 30–33)
2 tablespoons sugar
1 tablespoon lemon juice
½ teaspoon fine salt
½ teaspoon sea salt flakes

Pickled Cherries

1 x 400 g (14 oz) tin of pitted cherries
    in syrup, drained (save a little of
    the syrup and use the rest to make
    the Cherry and Tarragon Soda on
    page 138) and roughly chopped
1½ tablespoons caster
    (superfine) sugar
1½ tablespoons white,
    red or cider vinegar

SUBSTITUTES

Hazelnuts
almonds, macadamias, walnuts

Sugar
honey

As with savoury dishes, I like puddings to have a nice balance to them. Here's it's a good balance of rich chocolatey mousse, tart pickled cherries, crunch and depth from the roasted hazelnuts (filberts), and a little pinch of sea salt flakes. For chocolate is always better with salt.

If you're hosting dinner, this is a good one to make ahead of everyone arriving, as it'll happily sit in the refrigerator for hours, and I'm yet to meet someone who doesn't like chocolate!

* First, preheat the oven to 180°C (350°F/Gas 4). Roast the hazelnuts on a baking tray (pan) for 8–10 minutes, or until fragrant. Once cool, lightly crush in a pestle and mortar or with the side of your knife on a sturdy cutting board. Set aside.

* Meanwhile, melt the chocolate and butter in a heatproof bowl sat on top of a pan of lightly simmering water. Once melted, set aside to cool slightly.

* In a separate bowl, using a whisk, whip the egg yolks and sugar until pale, then mix into the melted chocolate. Wash and dry the whisk attachments so that they're squeaky clean, then whisk the lemon juice, fine salt and egg whites until you've got stiff peaks.

* Fold one-third of the egg whites into the chocolate mixture to loosen it. Gently fold in the remaining whites, taking care to keep as much air incorporated as possible so that the mousse remains light and fluffy. Transfer to a container (or six serving glasses) and chill for at least 2 hours.

* To make the pickled cherries, half an hour before serving, stir together the chopped cherries, sugar, vinegar and 2 tablespoons of the reserved cherry syrup. Set aside to lightly pickle.

———— To assemble

Spoon the chocolate mousse onto six small plates. Spoon over the pickled cherries, a scattering of crushed hazelnuts and a pinch of sea salt flakes.

COOK'S TIP

Don't throw away the cherry syrup. Instead, use it to make the Cherry and Tarragon Soda (page 138), or throw into the Bircher Muesli (page 63).

CARAMELISED BEETROOT, PICKLED CHERRIES AND WALNUTS

with Feta and Mint

SERVES 2
(OR 4 AS A SIDE DISH)

40 minutes

2 tablespoons rapeseed (canola)
   or light olive oil
bunch of beetroot (beet), skin on,
   thoroughly washed and cut
   into wedges
2 tablespoons sugar (ideally brown,
   but white is fine too)
½ teaspoon sea salt, plus a pinch
½ x 400 g (14 oz) tin of pitted cherries
   in syrup, drained and rinsed (save
   the syrup and remaining cherries
   to make the Cherry and Tarragon
   Soda on page 138)
3 tablespoons red wine vinegar
50 g (2 oz/scant ½ cup) whole
   shelled walnuts
3 tablespoons feta
4 sprigs of mint
small handful of dill fronds
freshly ground black pepper

SUBSTITUTES

Walnuts
almonds, hazelnuts (filberts), pecans

Feta
salted ricotta, manchego,
strong Cheddar

Mint/dill
flat-leaf parsley

Quickly pickling a regular tin of cherries here elevates a bunch of beetroot into a pretty special salad as their tart-sweetness contrasts so nicely with the earthiness of the beetroot.

If you have any leftover, try making the Chocolate Mousse on page 128, or the Cherry and Tarragon Soda (page 138), stirred together with some iced gin.

∗ First, add the oil to a wide pan over a high heat, then fry the beetroot for 8–10 minutes, stirring occasionally until beginning to catch and caramelise. Cover with 500 ml (17 fl oz/2 cups) of water, then add the sugar and salt and simmer for 25 minutes, or until the water is reduced to a sticky glaze and the beetroot is tender when you poke a knife into it. Remove from the heat and allow to cool.

∗ Meanwhile, toss the cherries with the vinegar and a pinch of salt in a small bowl. Toast the walnuts in a large frying pan (skillet) for 2–3 minutes over a high heat to release their natural oils (be careful not to burn them), then transfer to a plate and set aside to cool.

———— To assemble

Divide the beetroot and its glaze between two plates. Spoon over a few cherries and a splash of pickling juice. Roughly crush over the walnuts, then finely grate over the feta using a Microplane zester or fine side of a box grater. Finish by picking and tearing over the mint leaves (discard the stalks) and dill. Finish with a good grinding of black pepper.

SALT AND PEPPER CHERRY CRUMBLE

with Toasted Rolled Oats and Hazelnuts

SERVES 2

25 minutes

1 x 400 g (14 oz) tin of pitted cherries, drained, (juice reserved, don't throw it away!)
juice of 1 lemon
2 tablespoons dark brown sugar
3 tablespoons blanched shelled hazelnuts (filberts), lightly crushed
4 tablespoons whole rolled oats
½ teaspoon sea salt flakes
freshly ground black pepper (or Szechuan pepper if you have it)
a few spoonfuls of cream, lightly whipped with 1 tablespoon icing (confectioner's) sugar (optional)

SUBSTITUTES

Sugar
honey

Hazelnuts
almonds, walnuts

Sometimes after dinner you just need something sweet, and this recipe gives you a short-cut crumble using ingredients you're likely to already have in the house, removing the need to dash out to the shops in order to get a sugar fix. The salt and pepper might sound slightly odd, but I ask you to hear me out – they offer a nice savoury flavour to balance out the cherries' natural sweetness.

∗ First, heat a small saucepan over a high heat, then add the cherries, 50 ml (1¾ fl oz/3 tablespoons) of the cherry tin syrup, lemon juice and sugar. Allow to rapidly bubble and thicken for 10 minutes, then turn off the heat and set aside to cool slightly.

∗ Next, heat a wide non-stick frying pan (skillet) over a medium heat, add the hazelnuts and rolled oats and toast for 3–5 minutes, stirring regularly to make sure they don't burn. Transfer to a plate and stir in ½ teaspoon of salt and a few turns of ground pepper.

———— To assemble

Divide the warm cherries in their syrup between two small bowls, sprinkle over the topping, then eat straight away with the cream.

HAZELNUT FRANGIPANE CHERRY GALETTE

30 minutes, plus 1 hour for chilling and 40 minutes for baking

Pastry

150 g (5 oz/1¼ cups) plain (all-purpose) flour, plus extra for rolling out
¼ teaspoon fine salt
½ teaspoon sugar, ideally caster (superfine) or soft brown
85 g (3 oz) cold butter (salted or unsalted), cut into rough cubes
1 x 400 g (14 oz) tin of pitted cherries in syrup, drained (save the syrup to make the Cherry and Tarragon Soda on page 138)
1 tablespoon milk, for brushing
clotted cream or good quality vanilla ice cream, to serve (optional)

Hazelnut Frangipane

50 g (2 oz/scant ½ cup) whole shelled hazelnuts (filberts)
2 tablespoons butter (salted or unsalted)
70 g (2¼ oz/⅓ cup) sugar, ideally caster (superfine)
1 egg yolk
¼ teaspoon fine salt
2 tablespoons double (heavy) cream or full-fat milk

SUBSTITUTES

Sugar
honey

Hazelnuts
almonds, pistachios

After turning on the coffee machine, my first job at 27 Elliott's early each morning is to roll out the day's galette. We keep a big batch of almond or hazelnut (filbert) frangipane in the refrigerator then just top spoonfuls over the rolled out pastry, along with whichever fruit we have to hand. Here I've given you guidance for tinned cherries from the back of the cupboard, but you could easily use apples, pears, rhubarb or soft berries to make an impressive galette.

The brilliant thing about this pastry is that you don't need to be precious or have the daintiest patisserie skills; in fact, the rougher your shape, the more rustic and inviting it ends up looking! A slice of this galette on its own is a fine thing, but if you're going all out, some clotted cream or ice cream takes it to the next level.

＊ To make the pastry, rub the flour, salt, sugar and butter together in a large mixing bowl, using your index and middle fingers and thumbs, until you've got large, rough flakes. (Don't worry if some of your butter is still quite chunky.) Stir in a few splashes of cold water until the mixture is combined to a dough, then wrap in cling film (plastic wrap) and pop in the refrigerator for 1 hour.

＊ Meanwhile, to make the hazelnut frangipane, blitz the hazelnuts in a food processor until finely ground. Add the butter, sugar, egg yolk, salt and cream until combined, then set aside.

＊ Once the pasty has chilled for 1 hour, preheat your oven to 180°C (350°F/Gas 4). Lightly flour your workbench, then, using a rolling pin or a bottle, roll out the pastry to a circle, roughly 28 cm (11 in) in diameter. Don't worry about it being perfectly round or neat at the edges. Spoon blobs of half the frangipane mixture over the pastry, then scatter over the cherries, followed by remaining blobs of the frangipane. Roughly fold in a 2 cm (¾ in) border, pinch slightly to create a crust, then brush the edges with milk.

＊ Using a large fish slice, transfer the galette to a baking (cookie) sheet lined with baking parchment. Bake in the oven for 40–50 minutes, or until golden and crisp at the edges.

＊ Allow to cool slightly before slicing into six (as you would a pizza). Best eaten on the day it's baked.

COOK'S TIP

A batch of pastry will keep well in the freezer for up to a fortnight when wrapped tightly in cling film (plastic wrap), so it's a good one to have stashed away. Likewise, the frangipane will keep well in the refrigerator for a couple of weeks in an airtight container.

When rubbing the pastry, try not to overwork it as the lumps of butter and unworked flour are what will make your pastry nice and crisp. If you wanted, you could make the pastry in a food processor. Just pulse it very gently – you'll find it comes together in seconds!

CHERRY AND TARRAGON SODA

with (Optional) Gin

MAKES 6 DRINKS

10 minutes, plus 1 hour marinating

1 x 400 g (14 oz) tin of pitted cherries
in syrup, syrup drained and
reserved, cherries finely chopped
small handful of tarragon, leaves
picked and roughly chopped
5 tablespoons cider vinegar
(ideally a good quality one)
gin (optional)
ice and soda water, to serve

SUBSTITUTES

Tarragon
rosemary, thyme

Cider vinegar
red wine vinegar, white wine vinegar,
lemon juice

We're always experimenting in the cafe kitchen to see which seasonal drinking vinegars and sodas we can offer alongside our food menu. This one is a firm summer favourite; the tarragon imparting a sweet, slightly aniseed note to the cherries. You can drink this as is as a daytime soda or mix in with gin for a quick evening cocktail.

* Stir together the chopped cherries, syrup, tarragon and vinegar, then set aside for 1 hour to allow the flavours to mingle. Then, using a teaspoon, have a taste; you may want to add a splash more vinegar if it's on the sweet side for you. Bear in mind you'll be adding soda to dilute it.

————— To assemble

Divide the marinated cherry juice among six glasses, top up with ice and soda (and gin if using).

COND

M

ENSED
LK

SOURDOUGH SEMIFREDDO

with Orange Zest

SERVES 8
(FITS 1 LARGE LOAF TIN)

20 minutes, plus freezing time

½ tablespoon rapeseed (canola),
    olive or vegetable oil
300 ml (10 fl oz/1¼ cups) double
    (heavy) cream
1 x 397 g (14 oz) tin of condensed milk
2 slices of cooled toast, blitzed into
    rough breadcrumbs
1 teaspoon sea salt flakes
4 egg whites
1 tablespoon lemon juice
1 orange

SUBSTITUTES

Cream
strained yoghurt, crème fraîche

Orange
lemon

We get a daily delivery of beautiful Company Bakery sourdough to the cafe each morning and knowing how much work goes into each loaf, I can't bear to compost any unused pieces. Instead, I save up the stale odds and ends, toast then blitz them and stir them through this simple frozen cream for serving on sunny afternoons. Here I've used white sourdough, but pumpernickel rye from the supermarket works brilliantly too, giving you an even deeper, nuttier flavour.

*   First, lightly grease a large loaf tin with the oil, then line with cling film (plastic wrap).

*   Next, using a hand-held whisk, whip the cream until soft peaks form. Fold in the condensed milk, breadcrumbs and ½ teaspoon of salt. Clean and dry the whisk, ensuring the whisk attachments are squeaky clean. Then in a second mixing bowl, add the egg whites, lemon juice and ½ teaspoon of salt; whisk until stiff peaks form.

*   Next, fold one-third of the egg whites into the cream mixture to loosen it. Gently fold in the remaining whites, aiming to keep as much whipped air in the mixture as possible. Pour into the loaf tin, then freeze for 6 hours.

——— To assemble

When ready to eat, remove the loaf tin from the freezer and slice the semifreddo into eight pieces. Using a Microplane zester, zest the orange over each slice. Eat immediately.

MISO-SALTED CARAMEL

CARAMEL SAUCE

MAKES 2 JARS OF SAUCE

15 minutes,
plus cooling and shaping time

1 x 397 g (14 oz) tin of condensed milk
200 g (7 oz) butter (either salted or
   unsalted), cut into cubes
200 g (7 oz/generous 1 cup) dark
   brown sugar
3 tablespoons miso paste
2½ teaspoons sea salt flakes

INDIVIDUALLY-WRAPPED CARAMELS

MAKES 40 CARAMELS

35 minutes,
plus cooling and shaping time

SUBSTITUTES

Dark brown sugar
caster (superfine) sugar,
soft brown sugar

Aware that most households have a forgotten jar of miso sat at the back of their refrigerator, I wanted to create a recipe that celebrates the soybean paste in a new way. Along with sea salt, here, miso adds a touch of umami earthiness to this simple condensed milk caramel, making it a pretty addictive combination.

I've given you two ways to take the caramel: first, as a sauce for pouring over ice cream, seasonal fruit (page 148) or even meringues (pages 114–115). The second way is to reduce the sauce even further, giving you a toffee-like texture to roll into individual sweets. These are ideal as a pick-me-up with coffee or for taking along to a dinner with friends when you've forgotten to buy a present!

* First, you'll need to make the caramel sauce base. Combine all the ingredients in a wide-bottomed pot over a medium heat. Using a whisk or wooden spoon, stir occasionally until everything has melted, then increase the heat to high and stir continuously for 8–10 minutes until you have a nice, glossy, pourable consistency. Once slightly cooled, transfer the caramel to a couple of jars. Allow to cool before serving.

* To turn the sauce into a toffee-like caramel, first, fill a jug with cold water and line a large baking tray (pan) with parchment paper.

* Next, follow the steps above to make the caramel sauce, then stir continuously for a further 15 minutes until thickened to a toffee-like consistency. Test the caramel is ready by dropping a teaspoonful of the mixture in the jug of cold water. Leave for 30 seconds then using your fingers, check how pliable it is – if it's easily rolled into a chewy toffee, then remove the caramel from the heat. If the caramel is still too thin, reduce for a further few minutes.

* Transfer the caramel to the lined baking tray and allow to cool completely (this takes around half an hour).

* Once cool enough to handle, cut a few more sheets of baking parchment into 40 square wrappers around (8 cm x 8 cm/3 in x 3 in). Pinch a small piece of caramel then roll into a long, thin cylinder and wrap in the paper like a small Christmas cracker. Or, if you prefer, a square or round shape – whatever takes your fancy. Repeat until you have roughly 40 caramels.

If you don't have any miso paste, just follow the recipe as is and you'll get a lovely salted caramel.

Stored in sealed jars, the caramel sauce will keep for up to 3 weeks. You could also use caster (superfine) sugar or light brown sugar; the caramels will still be delicious, just not as dark and rich in colour.

(Please take care and don't be tempted to taste the caramel until it has cooled for at least 10–15 minutes as it will be incredibly hot and, as I've learnt, will burn the roof of your mouth!)

Stored in an airtight container, the caramels will keep for up to 3 weeks.

GRAPEFRUIT, SESAME OIL AND MISO CARAMEL

15 minutes

1 grapefruit
1 orange (blood oranges are nice
    when they're in-season)
1 tablespoon sesame oil
1½ tablespoons Miso-Salted
    Caramel Sauce (page 144)
4 tablespoons strained yoghurt
    (ideally full-fat)
1 tablespoon black sesame
    seeds (optional)

SUBSTITUTES

Yoghurt
whipped double (heavy) cream,
crème fraîche

Sesame seeds
hazelnuts, almonds, walnuts

I like to make this dessert at the start of the year when citrus fruits like blood orange and grapefruit bring a much-welcome injection of colour into the kitchen. Sesame oil tends to be used more in savoury dishes, but here I pull it out from the back of the cupboard to bring a nice balance to the zesty citrus, sweet and salty miso-caramel, and rich strained yoghurt.

* First, slice the top and bottom off the grapefruit and then carefully cut away the peel and white pith. Cut out the fleshy segments and transfer to a bowl. Repeat with the orange. Stir in the sesame oil and set aside for 10 minutes to marinate.

———— To assemble

Spoon the yoghurt over the base of two small plates. Gently spoon over the grapefruit and orange segments, then pour over the caramel sauce and sesame seeds (if using) to finish.

SET LEMON PUDDING

15 minutes,
plus 2 hours chilling time

3 leaves fine-leaf gelatine (about 5 g,
    but brands differ, so take a note of
    packet instructions)
1 x 397 g (14 oz) tin of condensed milk
100 g (3½ oz) crème fraîche (both full-
    fat and half-fat work well)
juice and grated zest of 2 lemons

SUBSTITUTES

Lemon
lime, orange

It's crazy how simple this panna cotta-come-posset pudding is to make – definitely one to have up your sleeve for whenever a few friends are coming over, as you can make it a couple of days ahead. If you've got some nice little glasses, you can pour and set the mixture into those, although I also quite like making one big dish of panna cotta and taking it to the table to scoop and serve up in front of everyone.

* First, take a good look at the gelatine packet and soften the leaves in cold water as per the instructions.

* Next, combine the condensed milk, crème fraîche, lemon juice and most of the zest in a large bowl. Once the gelatine has softened and bloomed, transfer the leaves to a small saucepan and gently stir over a low heat until melted. Stir in the lemony condensed milk mixture, then pour into a large dish or four individual glasses (roughly 150 ml (5 fl oz/scant ⅔ cup) capacity each). Refrigerate for 2 hours before serving, then scatter over the reserved zest.

COOK'S TIP

The chilled panna cotta will keep for up to 2 days in the refrigerator. If you wanted, some in-season raspberries, blackberries or strawberries would make a nice additional topping just before serving too.

CONDENSED MILK

VIETNAMESE-STYLE ICED COFFEE

freshly brewed coffee
(ideally quite strong)
ice
milk
condensed milk

SUBSTITUTES

Coffee
strong chai tea, strong black tea

I became completely addicted to this way of drinking coffee on a trip to Hanoi a few years back – and as soon as summer kicks off in the UK I get back into the swing of making them. This isn't a recipe as such, more of a guide for you to play around with the quantities of coffee and condensed milk to your taste. All I would recommend is to choose a coffee that's pretty strong, to balance the sweetness of the tinned milk.

* First, divide the coffee among glasses, top up with ice and milk, then stir in a spoonful of condensed milk. Stir then taste; adding in more condensed milk if you fancy.

CONDENSED MILK

COOK'S TIP

If you've got leftover condensed milk, save it for making the Miso-Salted Caramel on page 144.

ABOUT THE AUTHOR

Jess is self-taught in the kitchen, her flavours and straightforward approach inspired by time spent living in Sydney, London and Bangkok.

She is the founder of 27 Elliott's; a cafe, workshop and supperclub space tucked behind Edinburgh's leafy meadows. There she cooks a weekly-changing, seasonally-led menu, enjoyed by locals alongside good coffee, fermented sodas and natural wines.

Before opening 27 Elliott's, Jess worked as a food stylist on cookbooks, magazines, adverts and TV. Previous to that, she was part of Jamie Oliver's retail team, responsible for the chef's 1000-product food and homeware range.

Jess lives in a cottage in the Scottish Borders countryside with her husband Philip.

THANK YOU

I wrote, tested, styled and edited this book throughout an intense six months; juggling pasta nights, supperclubs, the Edinburgh festival and finding our first home! None of the above would have been anywhere near as enjoyable without the ongoing support of Philip, my family, friends and 27 Elliott's team.

These recipes are shaped by the beautiful customers that come together to make my little green space on 27 Sciennes Road a community. I've listened to what my regulars make most from *Salad Feasts*, noted what their favourites are on our menu and quizzed them about their midweek shopping and cooking routines. It's a privilege to have a job that involves getting nice people around the table to enjoy simple food, and it's my genuine hope that this book proves to be a useful resource so that you can do the same in your own homes, with your ownloved ones.

Philip. Nobody makes me as happy as you do. Thanks for choosing me as the one to be by your side – you'll get used to calling to me your wife one day! I'll never be able to thank you enough for everything you do for me, but here's to big breakfasts and long dinners together in our new home.

Claire and Den. Your belief in me to make 27 Elliott's a reality is something else! One day I hope to be half as supportive, loving and funny as you both are. Here's to our next adventures along the road.

Kate and Stu. Even from the other end of the country you make me laugh – thank you for your support. For stepping in to do the washing up, to delivering hundreds of eggs, to confusing the deliveries for compost, I owe you for the laughter!

Linz. There's only one Linzi Scobie, and I'm so lucky to have you. This is the book for you Linz, let's make this blog happen!

Ben and Tim. Here's to being closer together next year, engagement surprises and farm trips. I always feel your support and Australian energy, thank you for being the best. Memories of dinners with you pair are some of my most treasured.

Jono. I'll never forget opening Matt's studio door to see you standing there. You are such a treat and a talent, and I'm always excited to see what you'll create next.

Matt. What a joy it is to get to work with you; I'd do it every day if I could! From your inky blues to your signature shadows to your brilliant storytelling, you really are magic. Thank you for your belief in me, for the extra time and care and for the trips to Scotland.

Rosie. I hope this book makes you proud, Queen! What a beautiful mama you are – that little lady of yours is so very lucky.

˜ial. Your belief in my vision is such a good feeling, thank you again for making this book happen and for pulling the ˜ang back together! Your hard work and care for your ˜ry is hugely inspiring. I hope we get to collaborate ˜y more years to come.

Claudia. Mate! From the thorough testing, to the fun on shoot, for introducing me to Ayran, I owe you big time for your contribution to this book. Wish I could see you more regularly for roast chicken dinners.

The Munros. Thank you for always supporting Philip and I. I'm looking forward to rustling some of these recipes up for you at Claymires Lane.

Philippa. Your vision, creative feedback and support for my work has been so reassuring these past months. I'm so excited to get going on our project together!

Nicola. From painting, to spreading the word, and coming to all our events, you've been massively supportive this past year, thank you. I hope you enjoy making some of these!

Jackie. Thank you for putting up with our 5am shoot alarms! I really wish we lived closer so I could cook for you more. If only everyone had a fairy godmother like mine.

Evi O. Your creativity, playful touch and attention to detail genuinely blows my mind. I feel very lucky that we get to collaborate. Next stop, wine brand?!

Evi O Studio. You ladies are the finest in the industry, I look forward to sharing a bottle with you when I'm back in Sydney.

Col and Lou. Thank you for letting me set up camp at your place and making it feel like no biggie at all. Of all the sales reps in town, you are the best of the best!

Louie. You brought the best of goodies for us to play with – thank you for nailing it.

Team 27 Elliott's. Thomas, Rachael, Josh, Imogen, Karolina, Harris, Madeline, Louis, Rowan, Joe. Each of you have brought your own good vibes to the green walls here – thank you for the kitchen laughs.

ACKNOWLEDGEMENTS

INDEX

Published in 2019 by Hardie Grant Books,
an imprint of Hardie Grant Publishing

Hardie Grant Books (London)
5th & 6th Floors
52–54 Southwark Street
London, SE1 1UN

Hardie Grant Books (Melbourne)
Building 1, 658 Church Street
Richmond, Victoria 3121

hardiegrantbooks.com

British Library Cataloguing-in-Publication Data.
A catalogue record for this book is available from
the British Library.

Tin Can Magic by Jessica Elliott Dennison

ISBN: 978-1-78488-320-1

Publishing Director: Kate Pollard
Commissioning Editor: Kajal Mistry
Senior Editor: Eve Marleau
Designers: Evi-O.Studio | Evi O., Susan Le, Nicole Ho,
        Rosie Whelan, Karina Camenzind
Photographer: Matt Russell
Photography Assistant: Matthew Hague
Food Stylists: Jessica Elliott Dennison, Rosie Reynolds
Food Styling Assistant: Claudia Lazarus
Prop Stylist: Louie Waller, Rachel Vere
Editor: Sarah Herman
Proofreader: Kay Delves
Indexer: Hilary Bird

Colour reproduction by p2d
Printed and bound in China by Leo Paper Group